Family Walks in the Lake District
The Northern Fells

SYMBOLS
ON THE ROUTE MAPS

Route on motor road   Unenclosed

                                   Enclosed

Good footpath
(sufficiently distinct to be followed in mist)

Intermittent footpath
(difficult to follow in mist)

No path : route recommended

(Off-route paths are shown in black.)

Wall   Broken wall

Fence   Broken fence

Marshy ground   Trees

Crags   Scree   Boulders

Stream or River
(arrow indicates direction of flow)

Waterfall   Bridge

Buildings   Unenclosed road

Summit cairn ▲   Other (prominent) cairns △ △

Ordnance column ◻   Limestone clints

Contours (at 100' intervals) ···900···   Railway

Miles from starting point   ④

Abbreviations:

O.S. : Ordnance Survey
Y.H. : Youth Hostel

Heights of fells, where stated in the book but not
confirmed by the Ordnance maps, are approximate

Family Walks in the Lake District

The Northern Fells

Easy walks for all ages from
Alfred Wainwright's walking guides

Edited by
Tom Holman

FRANCES LINCOLN

Frances Lincoln Limited
www.franceslincoln.com

Publisher's Note
The fell pages in this book are taken from the Second Edition of A. Wainwright's *Pictorial Guides to the Lakeland Fells*, comprehensively revised and updated by Chris Jesty.
  Please bear in mind that fellwalking can be dangerous, especially in wet, windy, foggy or icy conditions. Be sure to take sensible precautions when out on the fells. As Wainwright himself frequently wrote: use your common sense and watch where you are putting your feet.

Printed and bound in China

A CIP catalogue record is available for this book from the British Library.

ISBN 978-0-7112-3406-2

9 8 7 6 5 4 3 2 1

Contents

About Wainwright 7
About this Book 9

1   Hallin Fell 14
    from Martindale

2   Knott Rigg 22
    from Newlands Hause near Buttermere

3   Sale Fell 32
    from the Pheasant Inn near Bassenthwaite Lake

4   Rannerdale Knotts 48
    from Buttermere

5   Binsey 56
    from Binsey Lodge near Bewaldeth

6   Grange Fell (King's How) 68
    from the Bowder Stone near Grange

7   Barrow 80
    from Braithwaite

8   Dodd 92
    from the Old Sawmill Tearoom

9   Castle Crag 110
    from Rosthwaite

10 Latrigg 122
    from Keswick

11 Causey Pike 136
    from Stair

12 Mellbreak 150
    from Loweswater

13 Angletarn Pikes 164
    from Patterdale

14 Catbells 176
    from Keswick launch or Hawse End

15 Low Fell 190
    from Loweswater

16 Walla Crag 200
    from Keswick

17 Heughscar Hill 210
    from Askham

18 Haystacks 218
    from Gatesgarth

19 Maiden Moor 234
    from Grange

20 Place Fell 246
    from Patterdale

Index 260

About Wainwright

The Lake District is well known for its literary history. Writers like William Wordsworth, Samuel Coleridge, John Ruskin and Beatrix Potter are forever linked to the Lakes and are the chief draw for thousands of visitors a year. All of them owe much of their creativity to this beautiful corner of the country, and all, in one way or another, express their attachment to it in their writing. But it is safe to say that no writer has chronicled the Lake District with as much affection and care, nor nearly so extensively, as Alfred Wainwright.

Like most of Cumbria's literary heroes, Wainwright was what locals call an off-comer. Born in Blackburn in 1907, he did not travel north to the Lake District until he was twenty-three, and like many people before and since, he was instantly entranced by what he saw – the open spaces, the fresh air, the pretty lakes and tarns and, above all, the majestic fells. He came back often after that, but it was not until his mid-thirties that he found the opportunity, via a job in the treasurer's office in Kendal, to settle in the area.

Another decade went by before Wainwright hit upon the idea that was to be his masterpiece – a complete study of the mountains of the Lake District. After breaking the area down into seven regions he identified 214 tops that he thought worthy of being called fells, and set himself a thirteen-year schedule to climb each and every one from every direction possible. At first he intended to record what he saw, in sketches and notes, for his own pleasure, but with the help of a local librarian and printer he was able to turn his first collection – his *Pictorial Guide to the Eastern Fells* – into a book. Sales took off, and the audience eagerly awaiting the next instalment grew with successive books.

Such a major survey of the Lake District is ambitious in itself, but it was the way Wainwright went about his task that made his *Pictorial Guides* so special. He prepared every page of his seven books by hand, each of them immaculately presented and ready for the printer's press without a scrap of type in sight. He wrote the books in his forties and fifties, all the time holding down a full-time job in Kendal, and his work was done with military precision, with weekends devoted to walking and weeknights dedicated to writing up his pages. Each book took nearly two years to prepare, and he finished the research for his last fell – Starling Dodd in the *Western Fells* – with a week to spare on his schedule. His *Pictorial Guides* are testament to his remarkable resolve and stamina, both out on the fells and at his desk, but they are much more than a simple directory of the mountains. Wainwright called the books his 'love letter' to the Lakes, and as well as being immensely practical companions they are full of opinion, humour and passion – an expert and exquisite series quite unlike anything else before or since.

It is now more than fifty years since the *Pictorial Guides* were launched, and the books have remained consistently popular and adored ever since. Wainwright wrote many more books about Cumbria and beyond before his death in 1991, and became a rather gruff television star for a while when his walks were filmed by the BBC. But it is his *Pictorial Guides* that are his greatest legacy, and it is proof of their timeless appeal that the books are as revered now as they ever have been. The 214 fells that he recorded have become something of a challenge for Wainwright fans and completists, and his work has inspired a host of spin-off merchandise and books – of which this is one.

About this Book

This is a companion volume to *Wainwright Family Walks Volume One: The Southern Fells*, and aims to do for the northern half of the Lakes what that book does for the south side. It selects the fells from Wainwright's various books that are most suitable for families, and outlines walks up and down each that are within the reach of children in particular. Each walk reproduces Wainwright's notes for that particular fell, comprehensively updated by Chris Jesty in his recent epic revision of the *Pictorial Guides* for their second edition, and is complemented by more practical details that families will find useful.

The walks have been chosen with a wide variety of criteria in mind. They offer a range of starting points so that families can find fells close to wherever they may be in the Lake District, though the emphasis is on popular destinations like Keswick, Borrowdale and the Newlands valley. They take in some of the most popular and family-friendly fells of the northern Lake District, like Latrigg, Catbells and King's How, but also try to spotlight some of its lesser-known corners, like Mellbreak and Low Fell from Loweswater and Binsey and Sale Fell around Bassenthwaite. There is wonderful walking across the northern Lakes, and this guide will take you both on and off the beaten track to places that will become family favourites. Parents who want to help their children to quickly bag a few Wainwright fells in a spare morning or day will find plenty to choose from here – as will those who wish to get maximum quality of views in return for minimum effort, or those who seek more substantial walking challenges.

The fells are drawn from across the *Pictorial Guides*, plus Wainwright's subsequent guide to *The Outlying Fells of Lakeland*, and as well as being inevitably something of a personal choice, the selection is heavily influenced by Wainwright's opinions. The walks take in some of his most favoured parts of the Lakes, including what he considered 'the loveliest square mile in

Lakeland' (the head of Borrowdale on the Castle Crag walk); and 'the most beautiful and rewarding walk in Lakeland' (the return along Ullswater from Place Fell). And it includes his most cherished fell of all, and the place where his ashes were scattered: Haystacks.

The walks try to allow for access by public transport wherever possible, though there are a couple of fells that require a good deal of effort and planning to reach that way. Many more can be linked to reliable bus (and boat) services though, and travelling this way is to be warmly encouraged – not least because it was Wainwright's favoured mode of transport while undertaking his research, but also because it reduces the number of cars on the Lake District's roads and saves on the spiralling costs of petrol and parking.

Whether travelling by car or bus, details of how to reach each walk can be found in the pages that precede each walk. These notes also explain a little more about the appeal of the fells and their suitability for families, and list some of the best things for families to see and do before or afterwards. As all parents know, having places close at hand where children can get something to eat and drink is vital if they are to be coaxed along their walk, so recommended cafés, pubs and shops are listed too.

Directions for a route up and down each fell are also provided. These usually follow one of the routes suggested by Wainwright, but seek to provide much more step-by-step detail than he had the space or inclination to provide in his original notes. In order to provide walks that are circular rather than straight up-and-down wherever possible, the directions sometimes make a detour from his routes on the return to the starting point. The details are fairly prescriptive in order that families may find their way as easily as possible, but those who prefer to tailor their own excursions into the fells can find suggestions for shortening or lengthening the walks in the introductions, or plot their own alterations using Wainwright's notes.

Each of the directions and starting points incorporate Ordnance Survey grid references that will help those carrying maps or GPS devices to track their progress and work out where they should be if they go astray. The walks are arranged in rough order of difficulty, beginning with a mile-long stroll up Hallin Fell and ending with a 7-mile round of Place Fell. Because this measure of difficulty is based on an imprecise assessment of distance, height and terrain, and because all families' walking abilities and enthusiasms vary substantially, it is worth skimming through the options before settling on walks that are right for you. And while the choice of walks has been made with inexperienced walkers firmly in mind, not all of the fells are suitable for all children. Most of the terrain provides easy walking, and severe hazards are avoided, but some stretches are tricky underfoot or particularly steep, and any difficulties or places where extra care is required are noted in the introductions and directions. In height terms at least, the walks in this book are generally a little more challenging than those from the volume for the southern fells, in line with the general opinion that the top half of the Lake District provides slightly wilder and tougher terrain than the bottom half.

Walkers should always follow a few basic precautions that will make for a safe and enjoyable time in the fells, like wearing suitable footwear and other equipment and packing lots of layers and supplies of food and drink. Keep a close eye on the weather forecast – but whatever it says, prepare for all eventualities as the climate changes so fast in the Lake District, especially up on the fells. Take a map and compass with you, and know how to use them, because even with detailed directions and Wainwright's sketches it can be easy to take a wrong turn, especially in mist. If you have them, take a mobile phone and GPS device too – but accept that they have limitations and do not rely on them alone for navigation or safety. Be realistic in what you will be able to achieve in your allotted time, and remember that walks almost always take longer than you think they will, especially with young children.

Parents are also well advised to equip themselves with some ideas for cajoling young walkers up and down the fells. These walks provide plenty of resting points and things that will hopefully interest children along the way, including variations in scenery, but even the most enthusiastic of young walkers is likely to flag at some point. A bag of sweets or other treats that can be handed out intermittently goes a long way towards pre-empting complaints; the line between incentive and bribery is a fine one, but most parents will not be too worried about the distinction when halfway up a fell in the rain. Telling stories – especially based on the things that children observe along their walks – is another good way to distract young minds from the toil, as is singing, which has the extra advantage of establishing a walking rhythm.

Above all, have fun. Walking is a wonderful experience for parents and children to share, and these routes provide a chance to enjoy both the wonderful fells and one other's company, as well as opportunities for fresh air, exercise and a bit of education along the way. Whether you have walked here many times before or are visiting for the first time, these twenty walks will hopefully fire your own interest and introduce the fells to new generations of walkers. This, of course, is just the start, and the riches of Wainwright's *Pictorial Guides*, still informative and pleasurable reads after all these years, provide further walking inspiration for years to come. But until young feet are ready to tackle grander summits, these twenty walks await to help you explore the joys of the Lake District – and as Wainwright often pointed out, smaller fells like the ones featured here often provide much more interest and pleasure than walks twice as far or high. I hope they give you as much pleasure as they have to my own family and me.

Tom Holman
Cumbria, November 2012

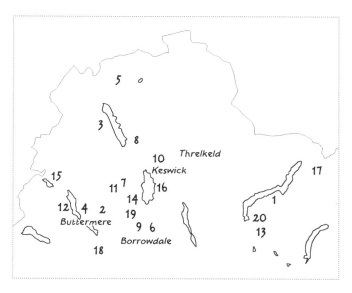

1 Hallin Fell
2 Knott Rigg
3 Sale Fell
4 Rannerdale Knotts
5 Binsey
6 Grange Fell (King's How)
7 Barrow
8 Dodd
9 Castle Crag
10 Latrigg

11 Causey Pike
12 Mellbreak
13 Angletarn Pikes
14 Catbells
15 Low Fell
16 Walla Crag
17 Heughscar Hill
18 Haystacks
19 Maiden Moor
20 Place Fell

1 Hallin Fell
from Martindale

For families wanting to notch up a Lake District fell with minimum effort, Hallin Fell could hardly be a better place to start. Of all the 214 fells covered by Wainwright in his seven *Pictorial Guides*, this summit is just about the closest to roads and civilisation, with the car ride up to the start accounting for much of the climbing and depositing walkers less than half a mile from the peak.

This is not to say a climb of Hallin Fell is without challenges. One of them is getting to the slopes in the first place, along narrow Lakeland roads that can be choked in summer and hazardous in winter. Another is finding parking, as the simplicity of the climb has made it very popular. And the sharp pull up, although very short, will have most walkers puffing and pausing for breath once or twice.

But the ascent is soon completed, and walkers get a summit and views that are far better than those achieved from walks many times as long. Or as Wainwright puts it in his notes: 'The rich rewards its summit offers are out of all proportion to the slight effort of ascent.' There are fine views back over the picturesque and peaceful valley of Martindale as you climb, and a panorama up and down Ullswater opens up suddenly and gloriously on the top. The summit is a great area for kids, with rocks to picnic on or scramble over and grassy knolls to tumble down, plus an obelisk that is one of the best cairns in the Lake District and can be seen for miles around.

The route described here, along the 'royal path' opposite the church, should not detain walkers for longer than an hour or two, and the way is so easy and hurdle-free that some families take a pushchair up, albeit with a great deal of effort behind it. Wainwright notes that sandals, slippers and bare feet have flattened the way up Hallin Fell over the years, but most walkers will prefer something with a bit more grip on the smooth slopes.

To extend this into a longer walk, add in a detour around the slopes to Howtown on the eastern side of the fell or Sandwick to the west, or pair the fell up with a ride over Ullswater to Howtown as described below. The roads beyond the church that wind further down into Martindale and Boredale, both of which are much quieter than the stretches from Pooley Bridge, make other pleasant short extensions.

From *Book Two: The Far Eastern Fells*

Distance 1 mile (1.6km)

Ascent 500 feet (150m)

Start and finish point The car park by St Peter's church in Martindale (NY 436 192)

Ordnance Survey maps Explorer OL5; Landranger 90

Getting there
The road to Martindale along the eastern side of Ullswater is narrow and, with lots of campsites and other holiday accommodation along the way, often busy. The only way into the valley is from the direction of Pooley Bridge; look for the turn-off before you enter the village. The final stretch between Howtown and St Peter's church is via steep zig-zags. The car park by the church has plenty of spaces, but they fill up quickly in the summer; there is some overflow parking by the roadside on the way back to Howtown. Parking is free, but donations towards the upkeep of the church are encouraged.

Martindale is one of the few parts of the Lake District not served by buses, with Pooley Bridge and Patterdale the nearest stops. But a good way to link the walk up to public transport is to take a boat over Ullswater from either Pooley

Bridge or Glenridding to Howtown. The leisurely journey around the lake takes about half an hour in either direction on splendid old steamer boats, and there are sailings every hour or so in the spring and summer, though services reduce in the autumn and winter. Check times in advance with the operator, Ullswater Steamers, to plan your day out (017684 82229, www.ullswater-steamers.co.uk).

From the landing stage at Howtown, follow the footpath west around the edge of the lake, then turn off left to follow it up the steep, zig-zagging road to St Peter's church; or pass the buildings to pick up a footpath beyond that winds round to the church. The boat can be linked up to public transport via the 108 or 508 buses between Penrith and Windermere and Bowness, or the 208 between Penrith and Keswick; all run to both Pooley Bridge and Glenridding.

Facilities, food and drink

The small and peaceful St Peter's church is left open for visitors and is well worth a visit before or after the walk. It was built in 1880 to replace the thirteenth-century St Martin's church, which still stands a little further down the valley.

The nearest food and drink is at the Howtown Hotel, run by four generations of the same family and with a walkers' bar and good afternoon teas in particular (017684 86514, www.howtown-hotel.com; open April to November only). There is more choice, plus shops to make up a picnic for the slopes of Hallin Fell, back at Pooley Bridge. Pubs include the Sun Inn, which has a children's play fort in the beer garden (017684 86205, www.suninnpooleybridge.co.uk), and the Pooley Bridge Inn (017684 86215, www.pooleybridgeinn. co.uk). For more ideas of things to do in the area, call into the visitor information point at the Ullswater Steamers office on The Square (017684 86135).

There are more shops and pubs at the other end of the lake in Glenridding and Patterdale. For a special occasion, try

Sharrow Bay, a legendary country house hotel and Michelin-starred restaurant between Pooley Bridge and Howtown – though only children over ten are admitted (017684 86301, www.sharrowbay.co.uk).

Directions

1 Cross the narrow road from the church car park and take the broad grassy path immediately opposite. It rises steeply straight away, and after about 100m forks. Take the right-hand path to continue climbing steeply with a wall on your left. After another 100m the path leaves the wall to continue climbing ahead. Ignore side-paths and follow the wide path sharply up – and don't forget to look back for fine views back down over the green valleys. After cresting a first brow, marked by a cairn, the incline drops a little. Again ignoring all diversions to stay on the widest, clearest path, rise up to a second brow, after which the path curves slightly right to the magnificent cairn on the summit of Hallin Fell (NY 433 198). Consult Wainwright's notes to identify the grand fells on the skyline like Blencathra and Helvellyn.

2 Continue on from the summit – the path bears right from the direction you reached it – and start to drop down towards the lake. After about 200m, where the path forks, do not follow it down towards crags over the lake (unless you want more views) but bear right to curve back around Hallin Fell, with Ullswater now to your left. Just under 200m further on is another fork, the left-hand path leading up to a cairn on a crag with more fine views over Ullswater and Howtown, and well worth the short diversion. Otherwise, continue on the soft grassy path around Hallin Fell until the church and car park come back into view below, then drop down to them on any combination of the criss-crossing paths set out before you. For a different route to your ascent, bear to the left of the church. Take care of children on this stretch, as the descent is steep.

Hallin Fell

1271′

from above Mellguards

Hallin Fell, beautifully situated overlooking a curve of Ullswater and commanding unrivalled views of the lovely secluded hinterland of Martindale, may be regarded as the motorists' fell, for the sandals and slippers and polished shoes of the numerous car-owners who park their properties on the crest of the road above the Howtown zig-zags on Sunday afternoons have smoothed to its summit a wide track that is seldom violated by the rough boots of fellwalkers. In choosing Hallin Fell as their weekend picnic-place and playground the Penrith and Carlisle motorists show commendable discrimination, for the rich rewards its summit offers are out of all proportion to the slight effort of ascent.

HALLIN FELL

● ▲
Sandwick Howtown

PLACE   ▲ BEDA
FELL ▲   FELL

● Patterdale

MILES
0   1   2   3

MAP

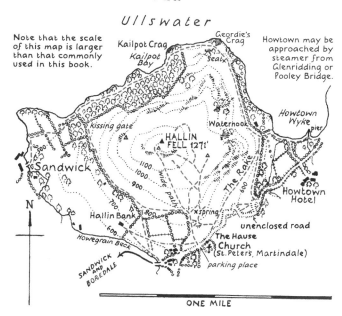

Ullswater

Note that the scale of this map is larger than that commonly used in this book.

Howtown may be approached by steamer from Glenridding or Pooley Bridge.

Kailpot Crag
Kailpot Bay
Geordie's Crag
Seain
Howtown Wyke
pier
kissing gate
Waternook
HALLIN FELL 1271'
Sandwick
1100
1000
900
Wide path
The Rake
600
Howtown Hotel
Hallin Bank
800
x spring
unenclosed road
600
Howegrain Beck
The Hause
Church
(St. Peters, Martindale)
parking place
SANDWICK AND BOREDALE

N

ONE MILE

ASCENTS

There is one royal road to the top: this is the wide grass path leaving the Hause opposite the church, and it can be ascended comfortably in bare feet; in dry weather the short smooth turf is slippery. Another track from the Hause visits the large cairn overlooking Howtown, and offers an alternative route to the top. Incidentally (although this has nothing to do with *fell-walking*!) the lakeside path *via* Kailpot Crag is entirely delightful.

HIGH RAISE   RAMPSGILL HEAD   THE KNOTT   REST DODD   GRAY CRAG   CAUDALE MOOR   LITTLE HART CRAG   DOVE CRAG

THE NAB   BEDA FELL   ANGLETARN PIKES

The Martindale skyline, from the top of Hallin Fell

THE SUMMIT

The man who built the summit-cairn of Hallin Fell did more than indicate the highest point : he erected for himself a permanent memorial. This 12-foot obelisk, a landmark for miles around, is a massive structure of squared and prepared stone. Built into the cairn is a plaque bearing various initials and the date 1864. A small cairn, with a good view of the twin valleys of Boredale and Martindale, lies 70 yards SSW.

The top is mainly grassy with bracken encroaching ; there is a good deal of outcropping rock.

DESCENTS : The temptation to descend east directly to Howtown should be resisted for the slope above the Rake is rough and unpleasant.

The easiest way off, and the quickest, is by the path going down to the church on the Hause. *In mist,* no other route can safely be attempted.

The lower reach of Ullswater from north of the summit

20

THE VIEW

Principal Fells

The bird's-eye view of Ullswater is dramatic, but the classic scene unfolded is an intimate one of green fields and steep fells, the Martindale district, for which this is the best viewpoint.

The panorama is good considering the modest elevation.

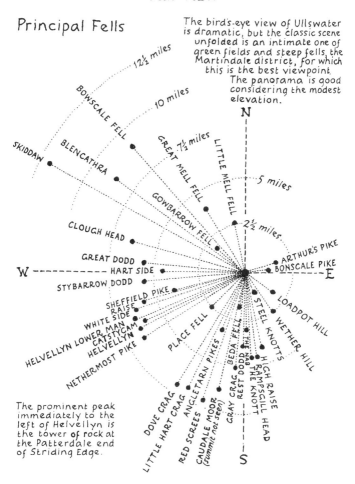

The prominent peak immediately to the left of Helvellyn is the tower of rock at the Patterdale end of Striding Edge.

Lakes and Tarns

WSW to NE : *Ullswater*
(all of the middle and lower reaches)

2 Knott Rigg

from Newlands Hause near Buttermere

Many fell walks in the Lake District require good navigational skills, but Knott Rigg needs next to none. This is a completely uncomplicated climb with the path up to the summit obvious throughout and, on a clear day at least, simple enough for children to take the lead all the way. At nearly 1,800 feet it is not insignificant in terms of height, but well over half of that altitude is taken care of before you even lace up your boots by driving to the start point at the Newlands Hause pass, so it should be within the reach of all but the youngest or most reluctant of walkers. 'This is a simple and straightforward climb,' notes Wainwright. 'A pleasant exercise, very suitable for persons up to seven years of age or over 70' – and, he presumably meant to imply, everyone in between.

Given the short distance of the walk and the popularity of the Newlands valley in general among drivers, walkers and cyclists, it is surprising to find Knott Rigg as peaceful as it is. Within a few minutes of leaving Newlands Hause walkers will usually find themselves enjoying complete silence, and the small ridge that leads up to the summit adds to the sense of isolation. Perhaps because of its modest challenges and the number of fells competing for people's attention nearby, Knott Rigg is often overlooked, but for families it makes a very good introduction to Wainwright's Lakeland fells. Together with Causey Pike elsewhere in this book, it is an ideal primer to walking in Newlands in particular, which was known to early settlers and tourists and extensively mined for centuries but is now one of the most picturesque but thinly populated parts of the Lake District.

As Wainwright, suggests, the walk to and from the summit will take only an hour or so at a good pace, and even with several leisurely stops along the way, no more than a morning or afternoon. To extend it a little, continue along the top to the second, slightly lower summit of Knott Rigg, or on to Ard Crags. This is an extra mile or so, and the fell is covered by a separate chapter in Wainwright's *Book Six: The North Western Fells*.

Alternatively, for a completely different way back, follow Wainwright's suggested route in reverse from Keskadale. For this way, retrace your steps a short distance from the top but very soon leave it to the left and look for a faint path running roughly in parallel with the one you came up on; turn left along it, soon bending away from the summit. If in doubt, strike to the right of posts that fence off a bog. The path soon becomes clearer as it runs along a heather-filled ridge, then drops down towards Keskadale Farm; turn right here for 1½ miles along the road back to Newlands Hause, or arrange for an obliging driver to pick you up. The route doubles the total distance of the walk and provides a bit of variety, but the roadside stretch back soon gets dull, and most walkers are very content to take the same way down as up.

From *Book Six: The North Western Fells*

Distance 2 miles (3km)

Ascent 720 feet (220m)

Start and finish point The parking spaces on either side of the road at Newlands Hause (NY 193 176)

Ordnance Survey maps Explorer OL4; Landranger 89 or 90

Getting there
Newlands Hause is on the road through the Newlands valley road that connects Keswick and Buttermere, just over 1 mile east of the village of Buttermere. It is one

of the most spectacular drives in the Lake District, and as such can get busy in the summer, so take care along the narrow road. Parking at Newlands Hause is free and spaces can fill up quickly, but there is room on both sides of the road and the turnover of cars is usually quick. Should you need it, there is more parking alongside the road just outside of Buttermere on the Newlands side, or in the village itself.

Buttermere is the village to make for if you want to link the walk up to public transport. The 77 bus runs on a loop from Keswick between early April and early November, four times a day both clockwise and anti-clockwise; both directions have roughly the same journey time as Buttermere is about halfway round the circuit. Walk up along the rather steep Newlands road from the village for the start of the walk.

Facilities, food and drink

Most people will approach Knott Rigg from Buttermere, which has a choice of places to eat including the recommended tearooms and ice-cream shop at Syke Farm (017687 70222). The village also has the Croft House Farm café (017687 70235) and two hotel-pubs, The Fish (017687 70253, www.fishinnbuttermere.co.uk) and The Bridge (017687 770252, www.bridge-hotel.com). Both can supply walkers with packed lunches. There are public toilets in Buttermere within the Lake District National Park Authority's car park. The village is a nice place to linger, and Wainwright fans can pay their respects at its pretty St James's church, which has a commemorative plaque and window looking out to Haystacks. At the other end of the Newlands valley is the Swinside Inn near Stair (017687 78253, www.theswinsideinn.com) and, beyond that, pubs and shops in Portinscale and Keswick.

If you have packed a picnic for the walk, the Moss Force waterfall makes an excellent place to enjoy it if the weather is too blowy on the top of Knott Rigg. It is visible from Newlands Hause and can be reached via a short stroll from the parking places in the opposite direction to the walk. As well as the falls, which are gentle by the standards of some in the Lake District, though impressive after rain and always attractive, there are pools for paddling and streams running off.

Directions

1 Leave Newlands Hause on the opposite side of the road from the Moss Force waterfall. Any route on to the small hill will take you in the right direction, but look for the grassy footpath at the Buttermere end of the parking spaces, signposted for Ard Crags. From the start the path is completely clear, with steps ground into the grass in places from the thousands of pairs of boots that have trod this way before. After about 200m it reaches a small grassy depression and, just over 300m further, a rockier plateau that leads on to a lovely small ridge with great views down to the valleys on either side. The next stop along is an outcrop of rocks sitting squarely on the path (NY 196 185), which can be skirted round to either side or easily clambered directly over if children prefer.

2 Once over the next grassy mini-top, the summit proper comes into view. The path leads directly to it, now over ground than can get marshy and squelchy underfoot. The highest point is marked by a small pile of stones (NY 197 189). The views are restricted by steep fells nearby, though it makes a nice resting place; keep an eye on children here as the drops off are steep in places.

3 Retrace your steps back to enjoy the ridge and the views again, followed by the rocks and depressions and down to Newlands Hause – or see the introduction to these notes for a longer alternative return journey.

Knott Rigg

1824'

from Buttermere

Keskadale is the long arm of Newlands extending southwest and providing the only outlet for vehicles from the head of the valley. The road is accommodated for two long miles along the side of a narrow and steepsided ridge of moderate height before climbing over a pass, Newlands Hause, formed by the gentle termination of the ridge; lovely Buttermere is beyond. This ridge has two distinct summits: the higher, overlooking Newlands, is Ard Crags; the lower, overlooking Buttermere, is Knott Rigg.

Sail Beck, coming down from the Eel Crag massif, of which Knott Rigg is an offshooting spur, very sharply marks the western boundary of the fell.

EEL CRAG ▲

Rigg Beck ●

▲ ARD CRAGS

● Keskadale

▲ KNOTT RIGG

⚡ Newlands Hause

● Buttermere

MILES

0   1   2   3

MAP

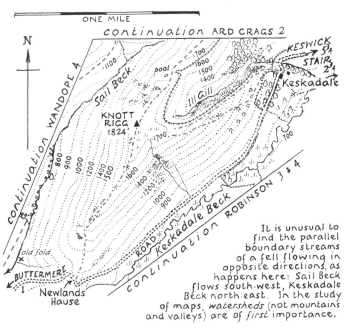

ONE MILE

N

continuation ARD CRAGS 2

continuation WANDOPE 4

Sail Beck

pool

Ill Gill

KNOTT RIGG 1824

KESWICK 5¼
STAIR 2¼
Keskadale

ROAD

Keskadale Beck

continuation ROBINSON 3 & 4

old fold

BUTTERMERE 1

Newlands Hause

It is unusual to find the parallel boundary streams of a fell flowing in opposite directions, as happens here: Sail Beck flows south-west, Keskadale Beck north-east. In the study of maps, *watersheds* (not mountains and valleys) are of *first* importance.

looking down to the *Buttermere* valley from the south end of the ridge, with High Stile and Red Pike in the background and the Newlands road descending across the side of Robinson in the middle distance

ASCENT FROM NEWLANDS HAUSE
720 feet of ascent : 1 mile

Upon reaching the ridge there is at once a fine view down the other side to Sail Beck and across it to the tremendous scarred wall of Wandope, Eel Crag and Sail.

Beyond the last outcrop the excellent turf of the ridge gives place to tougher grass, the summit being reached across a marshy plateau.

An advantage of solitary travel on the fells, greatly appreciated by all lone walkers, is the freedom to perform a certain function as and where one wishes, without any of the consultations and subterfuges necessitated by party travel. The narrow crest of the Knott Rigg ridge is no place for indulging the practice, however, whether alone or accompanied, walkers here being clearly outlined against the sky and in full view from two valleys. This comment is intended for males particularly. Women (according to an informant) have a different way of doing it.

Newlands Hause is commonly but wrongly referred to as Buttermere Hause

KNOTT RIGG

pools

summit now comes into view

outcrop astride ridge

grass

1500

pleasant grey rocks

1400

the ridge is reached between two small outcrops

1300

1200

grass

bracken

1100

depression

bracken

BUTTERMERE

parking area

1000

Newlands Hause 1096'

ROAD

Moss Beck

NEWLANDS KESWICK

looking north

Leave the pass at the waist-high signpost adjoining the parking area and follow the thin track that can be seen ahead climbing up to the ridge.

This is one of the few paths in Lakeland owing their existence very largely to motorists exercising their legs from cars left at the Hause, where the verges provide plenty of space for parking.

This is a simple and straightforward climb on the sunny side of the Hause, requiring an absence of one hour only from a car parked there. It affords a pleasant exercise, very suitable for persons up to 7 years of age or over 70.

28

ASCENT FROM KESKADALE
1000 feet of ascent : 1¼ miles

Upland *marshes* occur on almost all fells : on flat summits and plateaux, in hollows and on grassy shelves. They act as reservoirs for the streams, draining very slowly and holding back moisture to ensure continuous supplies independent of present prevailing weather. It is because of the marshes that the streams seldom lack water. They are safe to walk upon and cause little discomfort. *Bogs* are not functional. They are infrequent in Lakeland; there are no places bad enough to trap walkers, but some are a danger to sheep.

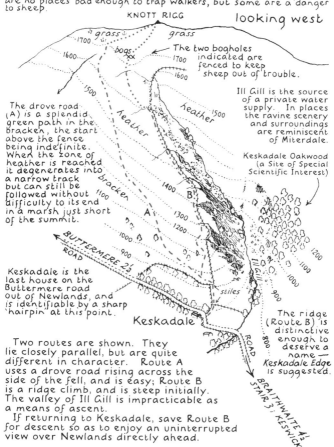

KNOTT RIGG

looking west

grass   grass

1700

1600

bogs
xx

1500

The two bogholes indicated are fenced to keep sheep out of trouble.

1700

1600

heather   heather

1500

Ill Gill is the source of a private water supply. In places the ravine scenery and surroundings are reminiscent of Miterdale.

Keskadale Oakwood (a Site of Special Scientific Interest)

The drove road (A) is a splendid green path in the bracken, the start above the fence being indefinite. When the zone of heather is reached it degenerates into a narrow track but can still be followed without difficulty to its end in a marsh just short of the summit.

bracken

1100

1400

B

A

1300

1200

1000

900

BUTTERMERE 2½
ROAD

Keskadale is the last house on the Buttermere road out of Newlands, and is identifiable by a sharp 'hairpin' at this point.

stiles

ILL GILL

1200

1100

1000

900

800

ROAD

Keskadale

The ridge (Route B) is distinctive enough to deserve a name — Keskadale Edge is suggested.

BRAITHWAITE 4½; STAIR 3; KESWICK 6

Two routes are shown. They lie closely parallel, but are quite different in character. Route A uses a drove road rising across the side of the fell, and is easy; Route B is a ridge climb, and is steep initially. The valley of Ill Gill is impracticable as a means of ascent.

If returning to Keskadale, save Route B for descent so as to enjoy an uninterrupted view over Newlands directly ahead.

THE SUMMIT

CAUSEY PIKE   BLENCATHRA

ARD CRAGS

There are two summits at about the same altitude and about thirty yards apart. The more southerly has two tiny cairns.

DESCENTS :

The simplest way off the fell is south to Newlands Hause, and the finest is via Keskadale Edge, but between these routes (assuming they cannot be located in mist) there should not be any trouble in going straight down to the road at the base of the fell. Sail Beck is rougher to approach and saves nothing.

Considering that it is clearly in view to travellers along the Buttermere road and conveniently near, the side valley of Ill Gill is rarely entered. It has many charming features beyond its father hostile portals and is worth a visit as far as a waterslide a quarter-mile in.

Keskadale Edge and Ill Gill

THE VIEW

Knott Rigg is so tightly sandwiched between the impending masses of Robinson and the Eel Crag range that an extensive view is not to be expected. The distant scene is not completely restricted, however, and eastwards there is a glorious outlook across the valley of Newlands to the lofty skyline of Helvellyn and the Dodds.

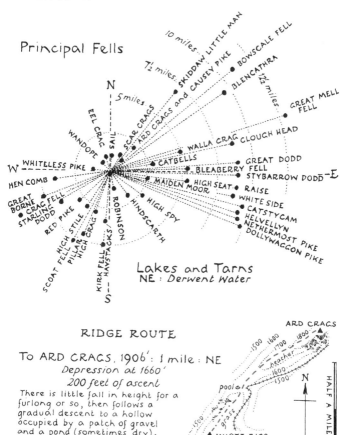

Principal Fells

Lakes and Tarns
NE : Derwent Water

RIDGE ROUTE

To ARD CRAGS, 1906': 1 mile : NE
Depression at 1660'
200 feet of ascent

There is little fall in height for a furlong or so, then follows a gradual descent to a hollow occupied by a patch of gravel and a pond (sometimes dry). Thereon a better path rises through heather to Ard Crags.

31

3 Sale Fell
from the Pheasant Inn near Bassenthwaite Lake

On the ratio of reward to effort, Sale Fell scores very high. A pleasant climb on easy paths with fewer than 1,000 feet of ascent delivers you to the top of this delightful fell in the north western tip of the Lakeland fells, just inland from Bassenthwaite Lake.

The lakeside railway from which Wainwright originally plotted this walk is no more, having been consigned to history along with many rural stations and train lines by the Beeching Report of the 1960s. Bassenthwaite's station was built in 1865 to serve Dubworth and other nearby villages, linking it up to Cockermouth and other towns in the west, and Keswick, Penrith and on to Durham in the east. It was built to carry minerals from the area as well as passengers, and survived for almost exactly a century – and for two years after Wainwright noted it in his *Pictorial Guide to The North Western Fells* – until April 1966, when the line ran for the last time. The ruins of the old station building can be glimpsed just north of the Pheasant from the A66, which was constructed over the station's old goods yard.

While the railway is gone and the A66 contributes a buzz of traffic noise, this remains a lovely, gentle walk. Starting from the Pheasant pub a few steps from the old station, it winds up a quiet road before branching on to and around the northern and western flanks of Sale Fell, before crossing its top and curving back round to the road. The broad and grassy slopes are ideal for children, who can run on to lead the way up to the top, and the summit has more open spaces that provide great spots for play or a picnic. They are usually empty, as Sale Fell's isolation means it doesn't get nearly as much attention from walkers as the fells further south.

Despite the walk's short distance, there is plenty to see along the way, including an example of the Lake District's small and lonely churches at the foot of Sale Fell (an older, ruined chapel is on the other side of the fell), and well-maintained woodland alongside the early and later stretches. See Wainwright's copious notes for interesting details about the wood and the Wythop – pronounced With-up – valley.

Sale Fell makes a fine morning's walk before lunch in the Pheasant or elsewhere, and it should be within reach of even small children. To shorten it further, to barely 1 mile in all, park at a lay-by where the path leaves the road up from the Pheasant, and join the directions at point 2.

From *Book Six: The North Western Fells*

Distance 2 miles (3.2km)

Ascent 930 feet (280m)

Start and finish point The free car parking spaces alongside the Pheasant Inn near Bassenthwaite Lake (NY 199 307)

Ordnance Survey maps Explorer OL4; Landranger 89 or 90

Getting there
The Pheasant Inn is just off the A66, near the north west corner of Bassenthwaite Lake. Look for a turn-off on the left towards the Pheasant and Wythop Mill just before the A66 bends away from the lake if arriving from Keswick and the south; or on the right just before you reach the lake if arriving from Cockermouth and the west. There is free public parking on roadside spaces in front of the Pheasant.

The Pheasant can also be reached by the X4 or X5 bus. This runs every half an hour or so between Penrith and Workington on the west coast, stopping at places including Stainton, Threlkeld, Keswick, Braithwaite, Thornthwaite, Embleton and Cockermouth. Penrith and Workington connect to the main north–south line and west coast branch line respectively if you are coming by rail, and the X4 or X5 links each of them to the Pheasant.

Facilities, food and drink

The Pheasant Inn at the start and finish of the walk has a very good reputation (017687 76234, www.the-pheasant.co.uk). It has a smart restaurant and a more casual bistro, as well as a bar area and a pleasant terrace. There are rooms to stay over, and a pool and spa. The hotel's afternoon tea is a particularly good way to end a walk up Sale Fell.

Other nearby places for food include The Wheatsheaf in Embleton, a family-friendly pub that is connected to the X4 and X5 buses (017687 76408, www.wheatsheafembleton. co.uk). Another five-minute drive west is Cockermouth, where the Tourist Information Centre on Market Street (01900 822634) is a good place to find out about things to do. The town's highlights include Wordsworth House on Main Street, where William Wordsworth grew up (01900 824805, www.nationaltrust.org.uk), and Harris Park and the Memorial Gardens, both of which have children's play areas.

In the opposite direction along the A66 is Keswick, which has plenty of places to eat, drink and shop, plus family attractions like the Pencil Museum (017687 73626, www. pencilmuseum.co.uk) and the Puzzling Place (017687 75102, www.puzzlingplace.co.uk). The Tourist Information Centre is in the Moot Hall on Market Square (017687 72645). Two miles north of The Pheasant along the B5291 is Trotters World of Animals, a wildlife park that has indoor and outdoor play areas, café and picnic tables as well as lots of animals for children to see (017687 76239, www.trottersworld.co.uk).

Directions

1 Looking towards the pub, leave the parking spaces to the right of the Pheasant, the way signposted for Wythop Mill. The quiet road soon rises, passing a Forestry Commission sign for Peil Wyke on your left. Wythop Wood is with you to your

left as you continue up to a cluster of houses at Routenbeck. Further up, where the road starts to level out and by some roadside parking spaces, look out for a track branching off to the left, signposted for Kelswick (NY 192 302).

2 Take this track, immediately passing through a wooden gate. Rise up on to grassy slopes. There is soon a bench from which to enjoy the views, and to the left as you look out is St Margaret's, a pretty church that can be reached for a short diversion. Continue up the slopes to a gap in a wall where a gate once stood. Carry on beyond, the grassy path now curving around the western flank of Sale Fell. It eventually meets a dry stone wall and bends left to follow it. After 60m with the wall on your left, look out for a path branching off half left (NY 186 296).

3 Take this path, and after 50m, where it diverges, follow the right-hand fork. The grassy slopes now rise steadily and pleasantly up Sale Fell; there are side-paths at points, but ignore these and follow the clear way to the summit (NY 194 297). There are wide grassy slopes to rest and play on. Use Wainwright's notes to help identify the fells in sight, including Skiddaw; the cairn that he sketched has now gone.

4 Continue on over the top to a subsidiary summit, then drop down beyond it on the grassy path. It leads in the direction of Skiddaw in the distance, and to the right of Wythop Wood. The path drops down to a gate; do not cross this, but turn left and continue downhill with the wall on your right. About 100m before it reaches a cross-wall by a gate, turn left on to another grassy path, through the bracken and with the A66 just visible ahead (NY 197 299). This path curves round the northern flank of Sale Fell, and drops down to a gap in a wall. Go through and bend left, with the church seen earlier now visible in the trees ahead and then reaching the bench. Turn right back down to the road, and follow it downhill to the Pheasant and the parking spaces.

Sale Fell

1178'

from the Wythop valley

Embleton
•

Dubwath
•

Wythop
Mill
•

▲ SALE FELL

LING ▲
FELL

● Beck
Wythop

BROOM ▲
FELL

▲ LORD'S
SEAT

● High
Lorton

Thornthwaite

MILES

0   1   2   3

NATURAL FEATURES

Sale Fell is the extreme corner-stone of the North western Fells, with an outlook ranging far across the west Cumbrian plain to the Scottish coast. It is a familiar sight on the busy Keswick-Workington road, of which it has an oversight for several miles; going west along this road, Sale Fell marks the end of Lakeland.

It is a pleasant eminence of low altitude, not remarkable in itself (although of some interest to geologists) and its main attraction to walkers will be as an easy promenade providing an aerial survey of the hidden Wythop valley. The fell is grassy, with bracken, but the eastern slopes, going down sharply to Bassenthwaite Lake, are within the boundary of Thornthwaite Forest, and thickly planted. This is an old part of the forest, long known as Wythop Wood, and there is a welcome blend of its natural growth of deciduous trees with the more-favoured evergreens introduced commercially in the twentieth century.

There is a significance in the name of the olde hostelry, the Pheasant Inn, at the foot of the fell. At one time this neighbourhood was actively engaged in the rearing of game birds and there were pheasantries at Lothwaite Side and in the Wood itself.

One very delightful feature of Wythop Wood is the presence of the lovely little roe deer, shyest of creatures. The new plantations are fenced off against them, but they have freedom to roam in the older woodlands, and the men of the Forestry Commission deserve a very good mark for tolerating and harbouring these gentle animals in their preserves.

Baby
roe deer

born to be free ?
or to be hunted
and snared and
shot by brave
sportsmen?

Roe buck

37

The Wythop Valley

The name is pronounced *With-up* locally. This quiet valley, almost unknown to Lakeland's visitors, is unique, not moulded at all to the usual pattern, a geographical freak.

The opening into it at Wythop Mill, between Sale Fell and Ling Fell, is so narrow and so embowered in trees that it might well pass without notice but for a signpost indicating a byway to Wythop Hall. Following this through a richly-wooded dell, the view up the valley opens suddenly beyond the farm of Eskin to reveal a lofty mountain directly ahead a few miles distant — a sight to stop explorers in their tracks. Of course all valleys run up into hills ..... but what can this towering height be ? .... Hearts quicken .... have we discovered an unknown 3000' peak ? Wainwright's map on page 8 indicates no mountain ahead .... Get out a *decent* map, the Ordnance Survey one-inch — and the truth slowly dawns ..... why, of course ....it's dear old Skiddaw, of course, not immediately recognisable from this angle ...... But how odd! What an illusion! The valley certainly *appears* to lead directly to the mountain, *but*, completely out of sight and unsuspected from this viewpoint, the wide trench containing Bassenthwaite Lake profoundly interrupts the rising contours in the line of vision. The fact is that the Wythop valley, like all others, has hills along both sides, but instead of the normal steepening of ground at its head there occurs a sharp declivity to another (and major) valley system, the Derwent, occupied here by the unseen lake with Skiddaw rising from its far shore. The Wythop valley, elevated 600 feet above that of the Derwent, drains *away* from it, and the unobtrusive watershed (a meeting of green pastures and dark forest) may therefore be likened to a pass. The whole arrangement is unusual and remarkable.

Having described the valley as a freak, it is important to say also, and emphasise, that its scenery is in no way freakish. *Here is a charming and secluded natural sanctuary in an idyllic setting, a place of calm*, where a peaceful farming community husband the good earth now as for centuries past. Every rod, pole and perch of it is delightful and unspoilt. Motorcars can penetrate as far as Wythop Hall but happily are unaware of this. The valley is undisturbed and quiet; red squirrels can still be seen. There are five scattered farmsteads and, at the head, Wythop Hall, rich in story and legend. In days gone by the valley maintained a larger population and a church.

The Wythop Valley

The Great
Illusion
(see opposite page)

Looking up the Wythop Valley to Skiddaw,
from the slopes of Ling Fell. The furthest
line of trees marks the end of the valley and
Skiddaw rises beyond the unseen Bass Lake.

In this view from Lord's Seat, the Wythop Valley is seen sloping
up gently from the left to the plantations of Wythop Wood, which
fall steeply to Bass Lake. The distant hill on the right is Binsey.

Ladies Table

In Wythop Wood

Ladies Table is a little peak at the head of the Wythop Valley above the declivity to Bassenthwaite Lake and within the forest boundary. Now wooded to the top at 950', it has lost its former reputation as a viewpoint. A flat boulder, probably used by Victorian picnickers, may have given the place its name, but more likely it is a gentle parody on Lord's Seat nearby.

All the paths in this area are completely overgrown or blocked by trees, and a visit is not recommended. The place is forgotten and only the name remains.

In the woodlands to the west of Ladies Table are numbered nesting boxes and life-size models of deer and peacocks.

The Walton Memorial
Perched on the edge of a crag in the heart of the forest, with a splendid vista of Skiddaw, is a memorial seat in native green stone, with a tablet inscribed "Thornthwaite Forest. In memory of WILFRED WALTON, Head Forester 1948-1959. In appreciation."

looking southwest

Putting out pipes and cigarettes, follow the forest paths from the cottages as indicated, watching for the first turn left in 250 yards. *Don't let the children go on ahead : DANGER!*

Looking across the Wythop Valley to Lord's Seat, from Lothwaite

Lothwaite is the eastern shoulder of Sale Fell. A grassy alp, it is a pleasant
sheep pasture and in summer is a floral garden. Apart from a solitary
boulder it is featureless. It gives its name to the farmstead of Lothwaite Side.
The suffix 'thwaite' is unusual for an open upland.

MAP

St. Margarets

At the side of a public bridleway beyond Kelswick is the crumbled masonry of a small building that would be passed without notice but for a tablet inscribed SITE OF WYTHOP OLD CHURCH against the inner wall. (On Ordnance maps it is indicated by 'Chapel—Remains of'.)

This old church has been replaced by a new one — St. Margarets — on the road between Wythop Mill and Routenbeck, but once a year a public service (necessarily open-air) is held in or near the ruins.

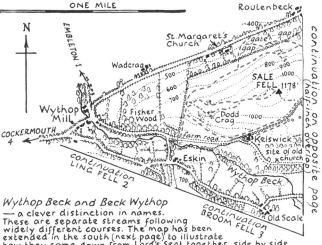

Wythop Beck and Beck Wythop

— a clever distinction in names. These are separate streams following widely different courses. The map has been extended in the south (next page) to illustrate how they come down from Lord's Seat together, side by side and almost arm in arm, until an insignificant watershed causes them to part company. Thereupon *Wythop Beck* proceeds to act as main drain for the Wythop Valley, escaping through a narrow gap at Wythop Mill to enter the broad strath of Embleton, and here it meanders, contrary to expectations, 'backwards' to Bassenthwaite Lake, joining it ¼ mile north of the Pheasant Inn (that's it at the top of the map, next page) after a circular tour around the base of Sale Fell. *Beck Wythop* has a much briefer passage, falling rapidly in its wooded gorge to join Bass Lake at Beck Wythop cottages.

Failure of an Enterprise

There is a story behind the ruins on the edge of the wood (south of Wythop Hall, map next page). Here are substantial foundations of buildings, and it is a great surprise to find them in so remote a place and in such rural surroundings. In the 1930's modern plant was installed here for the manufacture of silica bricks, a mineral railway laid, the road to Wythop Hall improved and re-routed and scores of workmen engaged. The product was not of sufficiently good quality. The buildings and plant were dismantled and taken away, the men dismissed and the site vacated. Today only the road-extension to Wythop Hall remains in use.

MAP

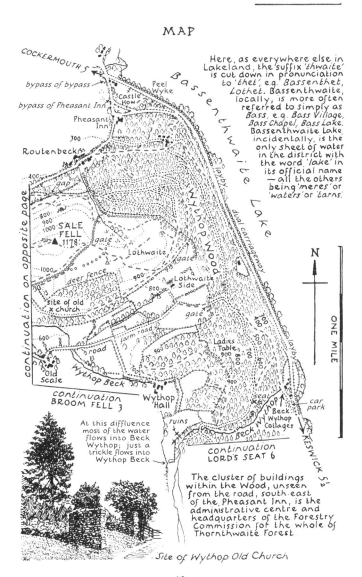

COCKERMOUTH 5

bypass of bypass

bypass of Pheasant Inn

Pheasant Inn

Routenbeck

Peel Wyke

Castle How

Bassenthwaite Lake

Here, as everywhere else in Lakeland, the suffix 'thwaite' is cut down in pronunciation to 'thet', e.g. Bassenthet, Lothet. Bassenthwaite, locally, is more often referred to simply as Bass, e.g. Bass Village, Bass Chapel, Bass Lake. Bassenthwaite Lake, incidentally, is the only sheet of water in the district with the word 'lake' in its official name — all the others being 'meres' or 'waters' or 'tarns'.

300

400

gap

800

1000

SALE FELL 1178

Lothwaite

1000

deer fence

900

site of old church

800

Lothwaite Side

gate

gate

Wythop Wood

layby

dual carriageway

N

ONE MILE

600

farm road

road

gate

Ladies Table 900

700

Old Scale

Wythop Beck

continuation BROOM FELL 3

Wythop Hall

ruins

800

900

layby

700 800

Wythop Beck

sea

Wythop Beck

Wythop Cottages

car park

KESWICK 5½

continuation LORD'S SEAT 6

At this diffluence most of the water flows into Beck Wythop; just a trickle flows into Wythop Beck →

The cluster of buildings within the Wood, unseen from the road, south-east of the Pheasant Inn, is the administrative centre and headquarters of the Forestry Commission for the whole of Thornthwaite Forest.

continuation on opposite page

Site of Wythop Old Church

ASCENT FROM THE PHEASANT INN
930 feet of ascent : 2 miles

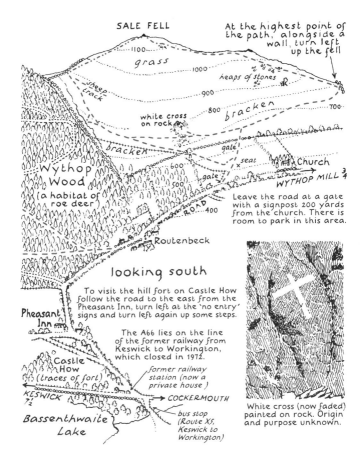

SALE FELL

At the highest point of the path, alongside a wall, turn left up the fell

1100

grass

1000

heaps of stones

sheep track

900

white cross on rock

800

bracken

700

bracken

600

gate

Wythop Wood

(a habitat of roe deer)

seat

Church

500

gate

WYTHOP MILL ¾

400

ROAD

Leave the road at a gate with a signpost 200 yards from the church. There is room to park in this area.

Routenbeck

looking south

To visit the hill fort on Castle How follow the road to the east from the Pheasant Inn, turn left at the 'no entry' signs and turn left again up some steps.

Pheasant Inn

The A66 lies on the line of the former railway from Keswick to Workington, which closed in 1972.

Castle How
(traces of fort)

former railway station (now a private house)

KESWICK 7½

COCKERMOUTH

Bassenthwaite Lake

bus stop
(Route X5, Keswick to Workington)

White cross (now faded) painted on rock. Origin and purpose unknown.

A pleasant little climb. Make a traverse of the fell by using both routes; preferably that on the left for ascent, that on the right as a way down. The round journey can be done in an hour from the gate at the roadside. Good views.

ASCENT FROM WYTHOP MILL
750 feet of ascent : 1½ miles

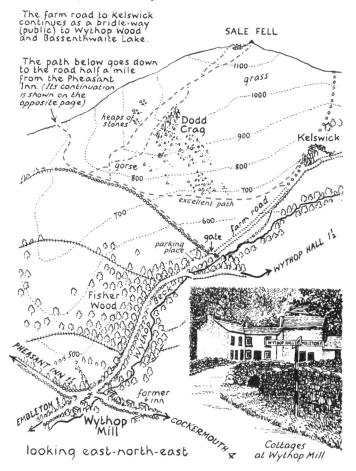

The farm road to Kelswick continues as a bridle-way (public) to Wythop Wood and Bassenthwaite Lake.

SALE FELL

The path below goes down to the road half a mile from the Pheasant Inn. (Its continuation is shown on the opposite page)

1100

grass

1000

heaps of stones

Dodd Crag

900

Kelswick

gorse

800

800

700

excellent path

farm road

700

600

700

WYTHOP HALL 1½

gate

parking place

Fisher Wood

BECK

WYTHOP

500

PHEASANT INN 1¾

former inn

EMBLETON 2

Wythop Mill

COCKERMOUTH 4

looking east-north-east

Cottages at Wythop Mill

A sylvan approach gives added pleasure to this simple climb. As an introduction to the Wythop Valley (an introduction warmly to be commended) this route is excellent and instructive.

THE SUMMIT

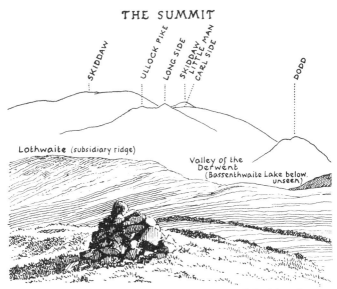

SKIDDAW
ULLOCK PIKE
LONG SIDE
SKIDDAW LITTLE MAN
CARL SIDE
DODD

Lothwaite (subsidiary ridge)

Valley of the Derwent
(Bassenthwaite Lake below, unseen)

The top is a pleasant grassy pasture populated by sheep but unfrequented by man — which makes it a desirable objective on a summers day for anyone who would like to visit a summit for quiet meditation without, however, incurring the expenditure of much energy on the ascent.

For ordinary mortals there is nothing of interest in the vicinity of the cairn, but visitors with geological knowledge might add to it by doing a little exploring. John Postlethwaite's excellent *Mines and Mining in the Lake District* contains this impressive paragraph:—
"Near the summit of Sale Fell, there is a small mass of very beautiful rock. It consists of a pink crystalline felspathic base, in which there are numerous crystals of dark-green mica. The base is chiefly composed of orthoclase, but some triclinic, probably oligoclase, is also present. There is no quartz visible to the naked eye, but small crystals may be detected under the microscope. There is also a little hornblende present. The rock is very hard and tough, and in lithological character is unlike any other rock in the Lake Country."   (with acknowledgments)

All this is Greek to the poor layman, and he would be no wiser after an inspection of three possible sites: (1) a rockface in view from the cairn, (2) a collection of upstanding boulders, and (3) a scattering of white stones, although he might notice that some of the latter appear to have been chipped by hammers. There is no other rock in sight, and one of these must be Mr. P's 'small mass', but, in spite of his liberal detail, *which*? What is 'orthoclase'? Or, worse still, 'oligoclase'? Resuming his

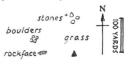

stones
boulders
rockface
grass
N
100 YARDS

meditations at the cairn after this abortive tour, let him now reflect on the poverty of his education. How much there is to learn about this fair earth and how little we know! How much beauty is never seen!

THE VIEW

The Skiddaw group is the best thing in the view, the top being displayed, not as the usual pyramid but as a long, level skyline. The Helvellyn range is also well seen as a tremendous wall running across the district, but elsewhere the prospect towards Lakeland is disappointing, the higher Lord's Seat nearby concealing the mountains of the interior. The Wythop valley below is very pleasant, a restful hollow of woodlands and green fields. Criffell is conspicuous on a Scottish horizon extending west to the hills of Galloway.

Lakes and Tarns
NE : Bassenthwaite Lake

Principal Fells

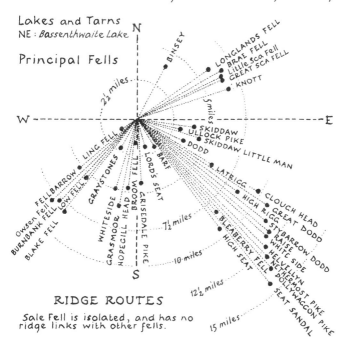

RIDGE ROUTES

Sale Fell is isolated, and has no ridge links with other fells.

A note for sheep fanciers :

The oldest strain of sheep in Lakeland is the Herdwick, a small, ragged but very hardy breed, tough enough to winter on the tops, and producer of the best mutton. Latterly, the Swaledale and the Rough Fell varieties, bigger animals with a heavier crop of wool but needing the shelter of the valleys in winter, have been increasingly introduced. The sheep on Sale Fell used to be a cross between Herdwick and Swaledale, combining the best qualities of each — but only in half-measure.

4 Rannerdale Knotts
from Buttermere

Buttermere is one of the Lake District's honeypot villages – a place to which walkers flock throughout the year. Its popularity is well justified, tucked as it is between two lakes, Buttermere and Crummock, and within striking range of a host of popular fells like Robinson, Red Pike and High Stile.

With so many good walks in all directions from Buttermere, and so many fells towering above it, Rannerdale Knotts is easily overlooked, but it offers a splendid option for families seeking a morning's or afternoon's excursion from the village. This, as Wainwright notes, is Buttermere's own local fell – its equivalent of Helm Crag for Grasmere or Latrigg for Keswick. It reaches only a very modest height, but has a fine rocky summit that makes it feel much higher, plus lovely views out towards nearby fells and, dizzyingly, down over the lakes. There is more to see on and from Rannerdale Knotts than on many Lake District peaks twice the height, and it is an excellent place for young walkers to get themselves acquainted with the fells. Wainwright calls it 'a mountain in miniature, and a proud one'.

As he notes, this is a fell with a more interesting history than most – at least according to local historian and publican Nicholas Size, namechecked by Wainwright. In a book called *The Secret Valley*, Size claimed it as the scene of a battle that saw Norman invaders beaten off by the native Britons, their knowledge of its crags and slopes and the adjoining valleys no doubt proving decisive. Local legend has it that the bluebells around Rannerdale sprang from the blood of the slain Normans. There is little historical evidence to support the idea that the Normans even reached this part of Cumbria – but it is certainly worth a detour to see the bluebells in the valley in the spring.

This walk up Rannerdale Knotts follows Wainwright's suggested route from Buttermere, which soon leaves the bustling village behind and rises up to a wonderful ridge,

Low Bank. This is a gentle, family-friendly ridge walk by comparison with many across the Lake District, but while it is short and at low altitude it makes for an exhilarating place to be, and children will enjoy leading the way along the very clear path towards the top. Further up, a rockstep requires some light scrambling that most children will find straightforward, but that makes the arrival at the cairn all the more rewarding for them. The return route is directly down towards Crummock Water, and this is a steep descent in places, with more rocksteps to negotiate. Families with young children may prefer to return the way they came up, which will add about ½ mile on to the total distance. Those with energy left to turn it into a longer walk can return the same way but then bear left at the col marked in the directions towards Whiteless Pike; it is a mile of steady but fairly straightforward climbing to the top from here.

From *Book Six: The North Western Fells*

Distance 2½ miles (4km)

Ascent 850 feet (260m)

Start and finish point The National Trust car park in Buttermere (NY 173 172)

Ordnance Survey maps Explorer OL4; Landranger 89

Getting there
Buttermere is reached on the B5289, which runs in a long loop through the north Lakes between Keswick and Cockermouth; or on the narrow road through the Newlands valley. The National Trust car park in the village is free for members and pay-and-display for non-members. There is plenty more parking in Buttermere, including the Lake District National Park Authority's pay-and-display car park by The Fish Hotel and some

free roadside spaces above the church. Some of the village's pubs and cafés have car parks of their own and may let you park for the walk if you eat there before or after, but check first.

Buttermere is served by the 77 bus, which tours a circuit from Keswick from early April to early November. It runs four times a day both clockwise and anti-clockwise from the town, via stops including Portinscale, Grange, Seatoller, Lorton and Whinlatter. Take the bus in either direction from Keswick as Buttermere is about halfway round the circuit, and ask for the National Trust car park stop.

To reach the walk's starting point from the village centre, turn left at the T-junction where the Bridge Hotel is on your left. The turn on to the footpath from the road will be on your right, soon after passing a row of cottages and about 50m before the National Trust car park.

Facilities, food and drink

Buttermere has several places to eat, including the tearooms at Syke Farm, which does very good ice creams in particular (017687 70222). This is a lovely place to camp. There is also the Croft House Farm café, which has baby-changing facilities as well as lunches and cakes (017687 70235). Two hotels, The Fish (017687 70253, www.fishinnbuttermere.co.uk) and The Bridge (017687 770252, www.bridge-hotel.com), both have public bars and will make up packed lunches for the fells. The public toilets in Buttermere are in the Lake District National Park Authority's car park.

While in the village, a short walk down to the waters of either Buttermere lake or Crummock Water is worthwhile, as is a visit to the small and picturesque St James's church. A window on the right has a stone commemorating Wainwright, with a framed view out towards Haystacks, his favourite fell and the place where his ashes were scattered. There aren't many family visitor attractions close by, but a 5-mile drive along the B5289 reaches the Honister Slate Mine, which has a visitor centre that highlights the history of mining in the fells and underground tours that children will enjoy (017687 77230, www.honister.com).

Directions

1 Turn right out of the car park along the road. After about 50m, cross the road with care to find a grassy path on the left, indicated by two public footpath arrows. Follow the direction of the arrow pointing up the slopes to rise up through bracken, very soon reaching a small wooden gate. Rise up on the grassy path beyond and, where it splits, take the right-hand fork, then skirting the rocks ahead to the right. There is a path directly over the spine of the crest that older children may prefer; they join up at the far end of the rocks in any case. Just under 100m after they meet, the path reaches a col (NY 179 177). Turn left here.

2 The way along the delightful ridge, Low Bank, is now completely clear, cutting a green swathe through the bracken. After a small dip, with lakes now in view on either side, the grassy climb gives way to a short scramble up rock to the summit area. Continue past the first rocky outcrop to a second, where a cairn marks the highest point (NY 167 183).

3 Continue on from the summit, the path bending to the right of further rocky outcrops and then dropping down towards Crummock Water. The way is steep in places, with vertiginous views over the lake and the road alongside it. Soon after the stony path gives way to grass it forks; bear left here, and, at another fork further down, left again, in the direction of Buttermere village and in parallel with the lake shore. After another ¼ mile the path drops down to a road (NY 168 177). Turn left here and walk along the road with care. After just under 200m, leave it to the left on a rough track that cuts off a stretch of road. When this returns to the same road, turn left and soon reach the car park on your right, or continue on for the village.

Rannerdale Knotts

- Rannerdale
▲ RANNERDALE KNOTTS
- Buttermere

ONE MILE

from High Rannerdale

Rannerdale is seen by most visitors to Buttermere ——but only as a farm and a cottage and a patchwork of fields on the shore of Crummock Water: a pleasant green oasis in the lap of shaggy fells, but unremarkable.   Passers-by sometimes tarry in the limpid coves of Crummock, or stroll along convenient paths in the bracken, but most hurry past, to or from Buttermere, unsuspecting that these few acres, now peaceful pastures, were once a scene of violent strife. Rannerdale has a lasting place in history as the setting of a fierce battle in which the Norman invaders were ambushed and routed by the English in the years after the Conquest.

Alongside the fields, and thrusting as a headland into the lake, is the abrupt and rugged end of a low fell that extends south-east for a mile, gradually declining to Sail Beck. All the excitement is concentrated in the dark tower of rock above the lake. Behind, a quiet valley isolates the fell from the greater heights in the rear.

This is Rannerdale Knotts, a mountain in miniature, and a proud one. Not even Gable has witnessed a real battle! And, what's more, our side won!!

52

MAP

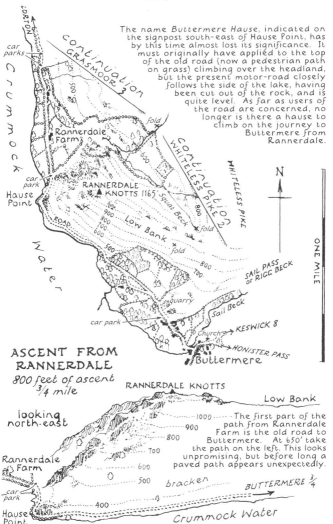

The name *Buttermere Hause*, indicated on the signpost south-east of Hause Point, has by this time almost lost its significance. It must originally have applied to the top of the old road (now a pedestrian path on grass) climbing over the headland, but the present motor-road closely follows the side of the lake, having been cut out of the rock, and is quite level. As far as users of the road are concerned, no longer is there a hause to climb on the journey to Buttermere from Rannerdale.

ASCENT FROM RANNERDALE

800 feet of ascent
3/4 mile

looking north-east

The first part of the path from Rannerdale Farm is the old road to Buttermere. At 650' take the path on the left. This looks unpromising, but before long a paved path appears unexpectedly.

53

ASCENT FROM BUTTERMERE
850 feet of ascent : 1½ miles

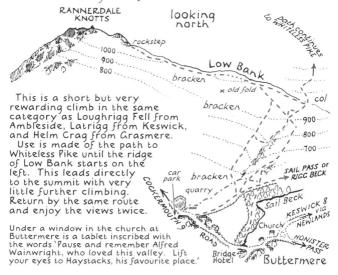

RANNERDALE KNOTTS

looking north

path continues to WHITELESS PIKE

rockstep

1000
900
800

Low Bank

bracken

× old fold

col

bracken

900
800
700

car park

bracken

SAIL PASS or RIGG BECK

quarry

COCKERMOUTH ROAD

Sail Beck

KESWICK 8 VIA NEWLANDS

Church

HONISTER PASS

Bridge Hotel

Buttermere

This is a short but very rewarding climb in the same category as Loughrigg Fell from Ambleside, Latrigg from Keswick, and Helm Crag from Grasmere.

Use is made of the path to Whiteless Pike until the ridge of Low Bank starts on the left. This leads directly to the summit with very little further climbing. Return by the same route and enjoy the views twice.

Under a window in the church at Buttermere is a tablet inscribed with the words 'Pause and remember Alfred Wainwright, who loved this valley. Lift your eyes to Haystacks, his favourite place.'

THE SUMMIT

ROBINSON

Newlands House

main summit

second summit

A succession of rocky tors athwart the narrow crest gives a fine distinction to this modest fell. Glorious views in addition make this a place for leisurely exploration. Rock formations and striations are interesting.

DESCENTS : The best way off is along the ridge of the fell, Low Bank, to Buttermere, and, after an initial rockstep just beyond the second summit, is a very easy stroll indeed. In mist, the road may be safely reached by a straight descent to Crummock Water from the depression between the two summits, but not elsewhere.

THE VIEW

The view is confined to a distance of a few miles only, but makes up in charm what it lacks in extensiveness; indeed the scene southeast, over Buttermere, is of classical beauty. Crummock Water is much better viewed from a rocky tower 80 yards west, beyond a natural dyke. A feature of interest is the 'hidden' upper course of Rannerdale Beck, directly opposite, the four bends greatly accentuated by foreshortening.

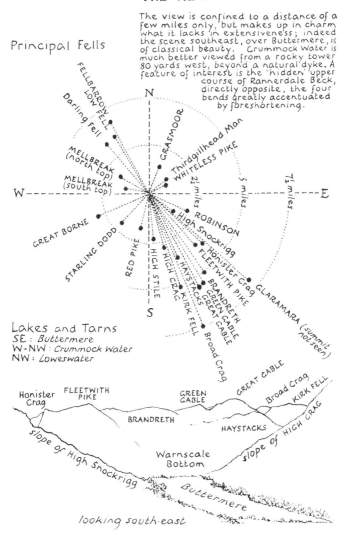

Principal Fells

FELLBARROW
LOW FELL
Darling Fell
MELLBREAK (north top)
MELLBREAK (south top)
GREAT BORNE
STARLING DODD
RED PIKE
HIGH STILE
HIGH CRAG
KIRK FELL
HAYSTACKS
GREAT GABLE
GREEN GABLE
BRANDRETH
FLEETWITH PIKE
Honister Crag
High Snockrigg
ROBINSON
WHITELESS PIKE
Thirdgillhead Man
GRASMOOR
GLARAMARA (summit not seen)
Broad Crag

2½ miles   5 miles   7½ miles

N
W — E
S

Lakes and Tarns
SE : Buttermere
W-NW : Crummock Water
NW : Loweswater

Honister Crag   FLEETWITH PIKE   GREEN GABLE   GREAT GABLE   Broad Crag   KIRK FELL
BRANDRETH   HAYSTACKS
slope of High Snockrigg   Warnscale Bottom   slope of HIGH CRAG
Buttermere

looking south-east

5 Binsey
from Binsey Lodge near Bewaldeth

Binsey is as far north as walkers in the Lakeland fells can go. With the northernmost of the lakes, Bassenthwaite, just below it, this is where the Lake District runs out.

Because of this far-flung position, Binsey receives few walkers, and its slopes are usually empty. This, of course, is all the more reason to pay it a visit, and it makes a peaceful contrast to some of the more popular climbs further south in the Lake District. The distance most people will have to drive to reach it is well worth the effort.

As Wainwright points out in his notes, Binsey is also unusual because of its separated situation. It is very much a hill in its own right rather than part of a range of fells – the final outpost of the Lake District, 'detached and solitary, like a dunce set apart from the class'. It has a distinctive, domed shape that is identifiable from miles around, and makes for an impressive sight despite its relatively modest height of less than 1,500 feet. And because it is unobstructed on all sides it provides a terrific viewpoint, with the sights extending on a clear day to the south as far as Coniston; to the north as far as the Solway Firth and the Scottish fells; and to the west out to the Cumbrian coast. To the east is Over Water, a large tarn that was dammed to supply nearby towns with water and is now looked after by the National Trust. For those approaching the Lake District from the north, Binsey makes a fine gateway, and the perfect place to survey the land beyond.

Although rather exposed on windy days, the grass and heather-covered slopes and rocky ridge at the summit are good places for children to explore and to linger with a picnic. The stones on the summit are from a tumulus, a Bronze Age burial mound that once adorned Binsey – a reminder that these slopes have been trodden for longer than we sometimes realise. The stones have now been put to more modern and practical use as a cairn and shelters.

This route up the fell combines Wainwright's suggested ascent from Binsey Lodge with a descent towards Bewaldeth, followed by a traverse of the slopes and a short section on a very quiet farm road back to the start. It is one of the easiest of all ascents covered by Wainwright across his seven *Pictorial Guides* to the fells, with well over half of the ascent taken care of by the drive to the starting point, and the way up to the top is entirely straightforward and within the reach of even the most reluctant young walkers. As Wainwright puts it of the Bewaldeth route up: 'This is a pleasant little climb at any season of the year, but on a warm clear day in August the purple heather and glorious panoramic view together make Binsey one of the best places for spending an hour of undisturbed peace and enjoyment. Or take the family.'

From *Book Five: The Northern Fells*

Distance 3 miles (4.8km)

Ascent 620 feet (190m)

Start and finish point Parking spaces by the roadside at Binsey Lodge, nearly two miles east of Bewaldeth (NY 235 351)

Ordnance Survey maps Explorer OL4; Landranger 89 or 90

Getting there

The starting point by Binsey Lodge is just under two miles east of the village of Bewaldeth. Follow the A591 from Keswick alongside Bassenthwaite Lake, and take the Bewaldeth turn-off, about 1 mile after passing the Castle Inn. Pass the cluster of houses in the village and then bear left at the fork in the road. Pass a farm and look for the parking spaces 1 mile further on, just before the road reaches a T-junction. Take care not to obstruct the farm gate on the roadside when you park. If the spaces are full, there are more along the road back towards Bewaldeth.

The walk can be connected up to public transport, but it takes a little planning. The 73 bus between Keswick and Carlisle passes very close to the start of the walk; ask to be dropped at Binsey Lodge, just before Uldale if coming from Keswick. There are only a couple of services a day between April and November, and on Saturdays all year round, but the timings should give you enough time to complete the walk. Another option is the 554 bus between Keswick and Carlisle, which runs a bit more regularly and daily all year round. Get off the bus at Bewaldeth and either follow this walk in reverse or take Wainwright's suggested route up from the village.

Facilities, food and drink

Binsey is usually climbed as a destination in its own right rather than because walkers happen to be near it, and there are few facilities close by. The nearest place to eat is in Uldale, where the seventeenth-century Snooty Fox Inn serves good food and local beers, though it is open in the evenings only (016973 71479, www.snootyfoxuldale.co.uk). A little further on to the north is Ireby, another attractive fell village, which has The Lion pub (016973 71460). To the south from the start of the walk is the village of Bassenthwaite, which has a good traditional pub, The Sun (017687 76439, www.thesunatbassenthwaite.co.uk).

The nearest towns to the walk are Cockermouth and Keswick, each about 11 miles away. Both have plenty of shops, cafés and pubs. The nearest attractions and activities for families are also a drive away. Popular ones include a good farm park back down the A591 at the north end of Bassenthwaite Lake, Trotters World of Animals (017687

76239, www.trottersworld.co.uk). Further down along the A591 is a popular osprey viewing platform at Dodd Wood by Bassenthwaite Lake (017687 78469, www.ospreywatch. co.uk) and, across the road from there, the home and gardens of Mirehouse (017687 72287, www.mirehouse.com).

Directions

1 Look for the wooden gate in the wall by the car parking spaces that gives access on to the hillside; there is a sheep pen immediately to the right. The grassy path ahead is very obvious, and continues to be as you rise steadily up Binsey. Don't forget to look back for the views as you climb, which gradually open up many of the northern fells of the Lake District. Further up the path cuts through heather and reaches the summit area, marked by an Ordnance Survey column, cairn and an old shelter (NY 225 355).

2 Continue on in the same westerly direction, making for a subsidiary cairn. After this the rounded top of West Crag is visible. Make towards this on the same grassy path, but at a depression ahead of it look for a crossroads of paths, and instead of heading over the crag bear right to veer around it. This path continues down in front of West Crag and passes an old pit before descending to a wall with a metal gate (NY 216 356). Do not pass through this, but turn left.

3 This path is faint in places, but clings close to the fell wall on your right, so the way is clear. After just under ½ mile, look out for a small wooden gate in the wall and pass through it. Drop down directly towards the middle of the farm buildings beneath you, where a public footpath sign by a metal gate shows the way on to the farmyard. Turn left on to the road, which passes through the farmyard, and continue along it for nearly 1 mile back to the car parking places.

Binsey

1466'

from Robin Hood, near Bassenthwaite

Private path in Binsey Plantation

Ireby
High
Ireby · Uldale ·
▲ BINSEY
· Bewaldeth

· Bassenthwaite

MILES
0 1 2 3

60

NATURAL FEATURES

Binsey is the odd man out. This gentle hill rises beyond the circular perimeter of the Northern Fells, detached and solitary, like a dunce set apart from the class. It is of no great height, is well within the category of Sunday afternoon strolls, has an easy slope just right for exercising the dog or the children, is without precipices and pitfalls, never killed or injured anybody, breeds hares instead of foxes, and is generally of benign appearance. Yet it is much too good to be omitted from these pages.

For one thing it is a most excellent station for appraising the Northern Fells as a preliminary to their exploration. For another, it is a viewpoint of outstanding merit. For another, it possesses a grand little summit with a once-important but now-forgotten history. For another, its rocks are volcanic, not slate as are those of all neighbour fells.

Binsey occupies the extreme north-west corner of the Lake District. Beyond is the coastal plain, then the sea, then Scotland; nothing intervenes to interrupt this sweeping panorama. What a domain, and what a throne to view it from!

the summit ridge, looking east

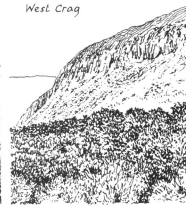

West Crag

MAP

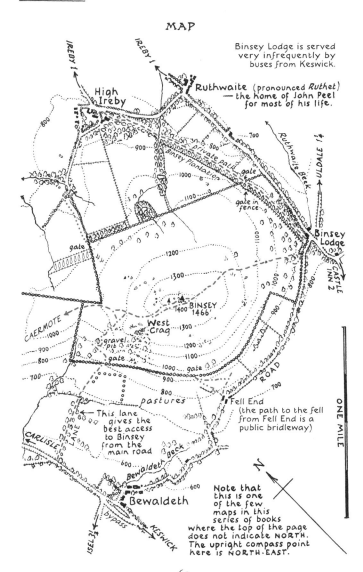

Binsey Lodge is served very infrequently by buses from Keswick.

Ruthwaite (pronounced *Ruthet*) — the home of John Peel for most of his life.

Note that this is one of the few maps in this series of books where the top of the page does not indicate NORTH. The upright compass point here is NORTH-EAST.

Fell End (the path to the fell from Fell End is a public bridleway)

← This lane gives the best access to Binsey from the main road

ONE MILE

ASCENT FROM BEWALDETH
950 feet of ascent : 1¼ miles

The summit of Binsey is remarkable for the ancient tumulus crowning the highest point: this is now accompanied by a modern cairn. An Ordnance Survey column stands between the two, and no fewer than four wind-shelters have been fashioned from the abundant stones of the tumulus.

BINSEY

West Crag

Path continues behind West Crag

heather

gravel pit

gate

The lane is a green avenue between trees, much cut up by tractors.

Binsey's outline is too smooth and gently graded to attract much attention, and its ascent from most directions is an easy trudge lacking in excitement. The route here shown is the best that can be contrived, bringing the few features of interest into view, notably the small cliffs and boulder slopes of West Crag. The rock here is a colourful volcanic, the whole fell being just outside the area of the Skiddaw slates, of which most of north-west Lakeland is formed

CARLISLE

MAIN ROAD

This lane, a third of a mile north of Bewaldeth, is the best (and the only direct) access to the fell from the main Keswick-Carlisle road

Bewaldeth

KESWICK

bypass

ISEL

looking north-east

This is a pleasant little climb at any season of the year, but on a warm clear day in August the purple heather and glorious panoramic view together make Binsey one of the best places for spending an hour of undisturbed peace and enjoyment. Or take the family.

63

ASCENT FROM BINSEY LODGE
620 feet of ascent : 1 mile

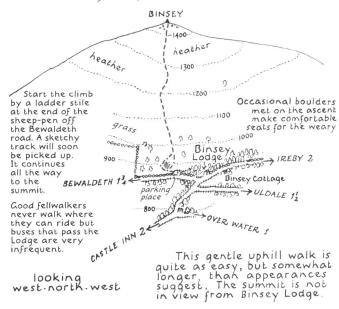

BINSEY

—1400—

heather

—1300—

heather

heather

—1200—

Start the climb by a ladder stile at the end of the sheep-pen off the Bewaldeth road. A sketchy track will soon be picked up. It continues all the way to the summit.

—1100—

Occasional boulders met on the ascent make comfortable seats for the weary

grass

—1000—

Binsey Lodge

→ IREBY 2

900

← BEWALDETH 1¾

parking place

Binsey Cottage

→ ULDALE 1½

800

→ OVER WATER 1

CASTLE INN 2

Good fellwalkers never walk where they can ride but buses that pass the Lodge are very infrequent.

looking
west·north·west

This gentle uphill walk is quite as easy, but somewhat longer, than appearances suggest. The summit is not in view from Binsey Lodge.

Binsey Lodge

ASCENT FROM HIGH IREBY
700 feet of ascent : 1½ miles

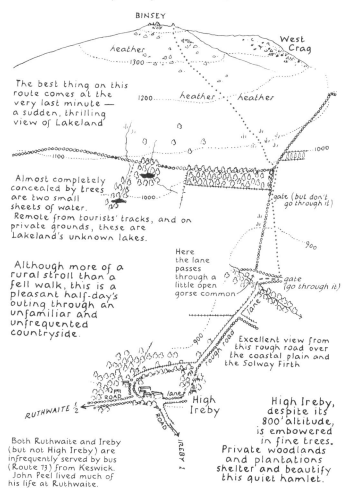

BINSEY

West Crag

heather

1300

The best thing on this
route comes at the
very last minute —
a sudden, thrilling
view of Lakeland

1200 .... heather ... heather

1100

1000

Almost completely
concealed by trees
are two small
sheets of water.
Remote from tourists' tracks, and on
private grounds, these are
Lakeland's unknown lakes.

gate (but don't
go through it)

900

Although more of a
rural stroll than a
fell walk, this is a
pleasant half-day's
outing through an
unfamiliar and
unfrequented
countryside.

Here
the lane
passes
through a
little open
gorse common

gate
(go through it)

lane

Excellent view from
this rough road over
the coastal plain and
the Solway Firth

900

rough road

RUTHWAITE ½

ROAD

lane

High
Ireby

ROAD

IREBY 1

High Ireby,
despite its
800' altitude,
is embowered
in fine trees.
Private woodlands
and plantations
shelter and beautify
this quiet hamlet.

Both Ruthwaite and Ireby
(but not High Ireby) are
infrequently served by bus
(Route 73) from Keswick.
John Peel lived much of
his life at Ruthwaite.

looking south-south-west

THE SUMMIT

The summit is the best part of the fell, taking the form of a small ridge surmounted by a great heap of stones (in fact a tumulus) with an Ordnance Survey column alongside and a modern cairn beyond it. The column bears a plaque dated 1999 saying that it forms part of the O.S. National G.P.S. Network. There is a lower cairn to the north-west. With the added attraction of an excellent view, this summit is worthy of a greater mountain than Binsey.

DESCENTS : All routes of descent are simple. At West Crag there is a little roughness. *In mist, bearings can be taken at the summit: the modern cairn is east of the Survey column.* Binsey Lodge (which is not in sight) is reached by aiming for Over Water (which is).

On the top of Binsey.........

..... Prehistoric Tumulus and Ancient Briton

THE VIEW

The Lakeland segment is only a third of the whole, but is full of interest, especially to the south, where again the surprising fact is demonstrated, by the unobstructed view of the faraway Coniston fells, that the central part of the district is generally of lower altitude than the perimeter.

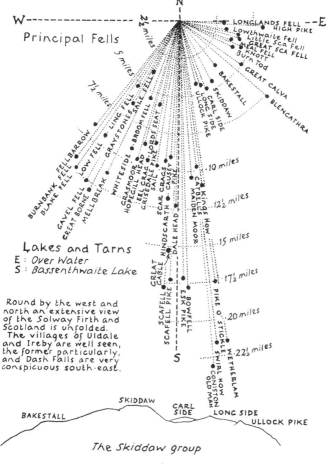

Principal Fells

W - - - - - - - - - - - - - - - - - - - N - - - - - - - - - - - - - - E

LONGLANDS FELL - - E
HIGH PIKE
Lowthwaite Fell
Little Sca Fell
GREAT SCA FELL
MEAL FELL
KNOTT
Burn Tod
GREAT CALVA
BLENCATHRA

BAKESTALL
SKIDDAW
CARL SIDE
LONG SIDE
ULLOCK PIKE

2½ miles
5 miles
7½ miles

BURNBANK FELL
BLAKE FELL
FELLBARROW
GAVEL FELL
LOW FELL
LING FELL
GRAYSTONES
GREAT BORNE
MELLBREAK
WHITESIDE
GRASMOOR
BROOM FELL
HOPEGILL HEAD
GRISEDALE PIKE
EEL CRAG
LORDS SEAT
SAIL
SCAR CRAGS
CAUSEY PIKE
HINDSCARTH
DALE HEAD
CATBELLS
MAIDEN MOOR
Kings How

10 miles
12½ miles
15 miles
17½ miles
20 miles
22½ miles

GREAT GABLE
SCAFELL PIKE
SCAFELL
ESK PIKE
BOWFELL
PIKE O' STICKLE
SWIRL HOW
CONISTON OLD MAN
WETHERLAM

Lakes and Tarns
E : Over Water
S : Bassenthwaite Lake

Round by the west and north an extensive view of the Solway Firth and Scotland is unfolded. The villages of Uldale and Ireby are well seen, the former particularly, and Dash Falls are very conspicuous south·east.

BAKESTALL   SKIDDAW   CARL SIDE   LONG SIDE   ULLOCK PIKE

The Skiddaw group

67

6 Grange Fell (King's How)
from the Bowder Stone near Grange

King's How has become something of a classic family walk – a first taste of the Lake District for countless walkers, and a fine day out from Keswick in particular.

It is more properly known as Grange Fell, of which it forms one of three separate summits. It took its name in 1910 on the death of King Edward VII, when it was bought in his memory by his sister Louise, who then gifted it to the nation via the care of the National Trust. A memorial tablet near the top marks out the donation of King's How: 'As a sanctuary of rest and peace. Here may all beings gather strength and find in scenes of beautiful nature a cause for gratitude and love to God, giving them courage and vigour to carry on his will.'

Wainwright shared the royal family's affection for the fell, considering it one of the overlooked gems of the Lake District, wrongly neglected by those seeking higher peaks to scale. 'In small compass, here is concentrated the beauty, romance, interest and excitement of the typical Lakeland scene,' he notes. This walk combines a climb up Grange Fell's northern side – 'a most beautiful short climb . . . in autumn, a golden ladder to heaven', thought Wainwright – with a descent to the south, though it can be easily extended to take in the fell's highest point, Brund Fell, if required. Most families will be content with King's How, which is the most attractive and interesting of the tops.

By starting close to the village of Grange, the walk also takes in a couple of interesting sights in the wooded foothills – a small cave that can be explored near the start and, near the end, the Bowder Stone, a huge glacial rock that was probably swept here during the Ice Age. Weighing around 2,000 tons and measuring 30 feet high by 50 feet wide, it is perched seemingly precariously on a point and is among the most photographed and visited sights in the Lake District outside of the fells and lakes. A ladder allows people to climb and explore it, though care is obviously needed with children.

From *Book Three: The Central Fells*

Distance 2½ miles (4km)

Ascent 1,050 feet (320m)

Start and finish point The Bowder Stone car park near Grange (NY 253 169)

Ordnance Survey maps Explorer OL4; Landranger 89 or 90

Getting there

The Bowder Stone car park is signposted from the B5289, on the left soon after passing the turn-off for the village of Grange. It is about 4 miles south of Keswick, the road passing alongside Derwent Water in between. The car park is free for National Trust members and pay-and-display for others. There is more parking in each direction along the B5289, and limited spaces in Grange.

The walk's start and finish point can be easily reached on the 77 or 78 buses, the popular walkers' services from Keswick. The 78 runs all year round, though less frequently outside of summer, and continues on into Borrowdale. It is usually an open-top service, which may or may not be an advantage in the Borrowdale climate. The 77 runs daily between early April and early November; take the clockwise service. Ask for the Bowder Stone stop on both buses, which will get you there in about 20 minutes. The return services run from the other side of the road.

Facilities, food and drink

The nearby village of Grange is well worth a visit before or after the walk, not least because it has two nice cafés for tea and cake: the Grange Bridge Cottage Tearooms on the left soon after crossing the bridge, with a nice terrace off the river (017687 77201); and the Grange Café, a little further up (017687 77077). There are public toilets around the corner from the Grange Café. The closest shops are in Keswick, and further down the Borrowdale valley are good pubs at Rosthwaite (the Scafell Hotel; 017687 77208, www.scafell. co.uk) and Stonethwaite (The Langstrath; 017687 77239, www.thelangstrath.com).

Other things to do in Grange include paddling in the River Derwent on the stone beach by the bridge and, very close by, the Borrowdale Story, a small exhibition housed in the Methodist Church. The displays tell the history of the valley, with particularly interesting material on the mining and farming that has sustained it over the centuries (www. theborrowdalestory.co.uk). Grange's second church, Holy Trinity, is a short walk up beyond the two cafés.

Directions

1 Drop down from the car park to the entrance and cross the road. Turn right along the footpath adjacent to the road, and after 200m look for an old memorial tablet on the opposite side (NY 254 171). Cross again with great care (the road is on a bend here, so find a better spot to cross if need be) and go through the wooden gate to the left of the tablet. Just over 100m on, at a crossroads of paths, go straight over to reach a cave, which can be entered. Return to the cross-paths and turn right to cut through bracken. Just over 200m on, the path joins another from the left to bear right and start the climb up King's How in earnest.

2 After crossing through a wooden gate higher up, it drops down slightly before rising up once more, now under cover of trees and over stone steps cut into the slope for much of the way. At a height of around 1,000 feet it emerges out of the trees; this is a good place to rest. Climbing again, the path joins a fence on your left for a short while, before bending away to the right. Follow the clear path up, bending left to follow the main route where it forks and scrambling briefly over rocks. This gives way to a final stretch through heather up to the rocky outcrops on the top of King's How (NY 258 167).

3 From the summit, pick up the path that aims directly for the lake for a few steps but then bends to the right. Within 40m you should pass on your right a memorial stone laid for King Edward VII. About 20m further on the path reaches a small cairn; bear left here. The lake is again in view ahead for the next 100m as the path strikes through heather, before dropping down over rocks to trees and bracken, and then down to a flat marshy area with crags ahead over the far side. Bear right here to skirt along the side of the marshy stretch. The path gradually gets closer to a fence on the left, and then meets it by a stile. Do not cross this, but continue on the path that bears slightly right ahead towards crags and, 20m on, leave it to the left on a path through bracken. The way can be obscured in parts by high bracken, but the fence remains close by on your left as a guide.

4 After about 300m the path approaches a gap in a dry stone wall; do not go through this but bear right. Again the way is faint in places, but the wall remains close by for a while before the path leaves the bracken behind to drop down to another gap in a wall. The path now winds down pleasantly through more bracken for just over 300m to a stile in a fence by the road (NY 255 161). Cross the stile and, with care, the road. Turn right along the roadside path, but just under 100m further on cross the road again to pick up a footpath, signposted for the Bowder Stone. It soon reaches the impressive stone. Continue on the easy stone path for about ¼ mile back down to the road, then immediately up the steps ahead to the car park.

Grange Fell

1363'

King's How, from Shepherds Crag

Grange Fell is nothing on the map, everything when beneath one's feet. In small compass, here is concentrated the beauty, romance, interest and excitement of the typical Lakeland scene. Here Nature has given of her very best and produced a loveliness that is exquisite. Not strictly the territory of fellwalkers, perhaps; yet those who consistently hurry past Grange Fell to get to grips with the Scafells and Gable would do well to turn aside to it once in a while, alone, and quietly walk its sylvan glades and heathery top. The exercise will not tire the limbs, but it will do the heart and spirit and faith of the walker a power of good, and gladden his eye exceedingly.

Rising abruptly between Borrowdale and Watendlath Beck, and split by that delightful little valley of trees, Troutdale, the fell is almost encircled by a grey girdle of crags half-hidden in rich foliage; below is the wreckage of centuries in the form of masses of boulders (one of which, the Bowder Stone, is famous) overgrown by lush bracken and screened by a forest of birches. The top of the fell is an up-and-down tangled plateau, from which rise three main summits: (1) Brund Fell, the highest; (2) King's How, deservedly the best-known; and (3) Ether Knott behind a barricade of long heather.

Lodore
HIGH
▲ SEAT

Grange ●
▲ GRANGE FELL

● Watendlath

Rosthwaite

MILES
0   1   2   3

MAP

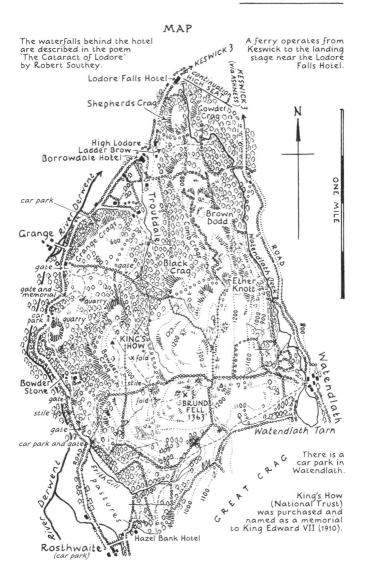

The waterfalls behind the hotel are described in the poem 'The Cataract of Lodore' by Robert Southey.

A ferry operates from Keswick to the landing stage near the Lodore Falls Hotel.

Lodore Falls Hotel

KESWICK 3

continuation HIGH SEAT

KESWICK 3 (via ASHNESS)

Shepherds Crag

Gowder Crag

High Lodore
Ladder Brow
Borrowdale Hotel

N

car park

River Derwent

Troutdale

Comb Crag

Brown Dodd

ONE MILE

Grange

Grange Crags

Black Crag

gate

gate

gate and memorial

quarry

quarry

car park

Ether Knott

Watendlath Beck

ROAD

KING'S HOW
× fold

Bowder Stone

gate

stile

fold

BRUND FELL 1363'

Watendlath

gate

stile

car park and gate

River Derwent

road

Frith Gill

pastures

Watendlath Tarn

GREAT CRAG

There is a car park in Watendlath.

King's How (National Trust) was purchased and named as a memorial to King Edward VII (1910).

Hazel Bank Hotel

Rosthwaite (car park)

ASCENT FROM GRANGE
1300 feet of ascent
(1050, to King's How only)
2 miles; 2½ via Troutdale
(1¼ and 2 to King's How only)

BRUND FELL

1300

1200

heather

Watch for the sharp turn left

old sheepfold

stile

1100

old sheepfold

heather

Long Moss

Black Crag

1000

900

800

700

600

500

boulders

gate

gate

gate

700

birches

500

400

gate

gate

600

Grange Crags

500

400

300

Comb Gill

300

Troutdale Cottages

500

400

300

car park

Derwent House

River Derwent

Grange

KESWICK 3¾

KING'S HOW

1200

1100

yew

Greatend Crag

Bowder Crag

ROSTHWAITE 2

800

700

Troutdale

The ascent is usually made from the road south of Grange Bridge. The natural line of ascent, however, lies up the hidden little valley of Troutdale

Every one of these trees has been drawn with affection: they make a wonderful display. Witness here how Nature arranges her plantings, and compare with Whinlatter and Thirlmere and Ennerdale!

Take the first path on the left beyond Grange Bridge, and avoid all tracks branching off it.

looking south-south-east

A most beautiful short climb. The first part, to King's How, is exquisitely lovely (in autumn, a golden ladder to heaven) and simply must not be missed. Sacrifice any other walk, if need be, but not this!

74

ASCENT FROM ROSTHWAITE

1100 feet of ascent to Brund Fell : 1½ or 2 miles
(1000 feet, 1½ miles, to King's How direct)

BRUND FELL

KING'S HOW

1300
heather
1200

1200

Bowder
Crag

1100

sheepfold
stiles

Follow closely
the line of cairns
(especially
in descent)

1100

1000

900

1000

800

900

700

800

gap

bracken

400

bracken

gate

bridle
path

gate

stile

gate

WATENDLATH

KESWICK

500

gate

gate

600

gate

car park
and gate

Frith Wood

Frith Gill

Yew
Crag

Note
here the
water-depth
indicators
on the side
of the road,
which is
liable to
flooding

500

River Derwent

Stonethwaite
Beck

ROAD

400

Hazel Bank
Hotel

Rosthwaite
(car park)

*Instead of using the
familiar Watendlath
path, try the quieter
way in Frith Wood.
The bridle path above
it is neglected and, in
summer and autumn,
choked with bracken.*

looking north

The diagram gives separate routes for Brund Fell
and King's How: if both summits are visited, as they
should be, the alternative may be used for descent;
the easier way round is to climb Brund Fell first.
This is an excellent little expedition, with splendid
views, but is not suitable for a day of bad weather.

ASCENT FROM WATENDLATH
550 feet of ascent : 1 mile (to Brund Fell only)

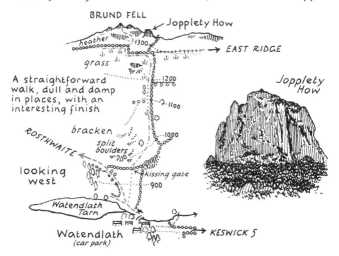

BRUND FELL — Jopplety How

heather · 1300

— EAST RIDGE

grass

A straightforward walk, dull and damp in places, with an interesting finish

Jopplety How

1200

1100

ROSTHWAITE

bracken

split boulders

1000

looking west

kissing gate

900

Watendlath Tarn

Watendlath (car park)

— KESWICK 5

THE EAST RIDGE

The east ridge of Grange Fell is not often visited, but gives an interesting and beautiful traverse, better done from south to north. The ridge starts to take shape at Jopplety How and a fence may be followed over marshy ground (no path) to Ether Knott, the most prominent peak on the ridge, which here alters its character and becomes rough and heathery, a wall taking over the duties of the fence; the easiest walking is beside it. Beyond, on Brown Dodd, the wall ends abruptly on the edge of crags, and there follows a sporting crossing of very steep ground. Escape from the escarpments hereabouts is effected down a rough gully leading to a pathless area where progress is hampered in summer by high bracken. Eventually the tourist path descending Ladder Brow to High Lodore is met, but having come so far the walker should certainly complete the ridge by visiting the top of Shepherds Crag, a lovely belvedere occasionally profaned by the rich language of climbers on the cliff directly below; on this part of the route again high bracken can present a problem.

Both sides of the east ridge have steep crags, continuous in the middle section. Overlooking the valley of Watendlath Beck is the gloomy wall of Caffell Side, while Comb Crags extend in an unbroken line above the trees of Troutdale.

The ridge is easily accessible from Brund Fell, but to force a way to it direct from King's How involves a laborious struggle in a tangle of thick heather. It offers a good return route to Grange or Lodore from Brund Fell (in clear weather) but not for pedestrians who prefer simple walking on distinct paths.

THE SUMMIT

The summit of BRUND FELL is one of exceptional interest. A number of steep-sided rock towers rise oddly from the heathery top; enthusiastic rock-scramblers will enjoy sampling them all, while less active walkers will find much fascinating detail in a perambulation of this unusual summit. There is no longer a cairn.

SKIDDAW

Derwent Water

The summit of KING'S HOW, in contrast, is a steep-sided dome, rising abruptly to a bare top with a small cairn.

DESCENTS: King's How is so encircled by craggy ground that descent by the paths is imperative even in the best of weather. To find the start of the path to Grange, head in the direction of Derwent Water: the Rosthwaite path leaves in the opposite direction (south) where an indistinct path is found. Brund Fell, too, is better descended by its paths, intermittent though they are, but in bad weather a safe and quick way to the Rosthwaite-Watendlath path may be made alongside the wall running south from Joppeltty How, first crossing it.

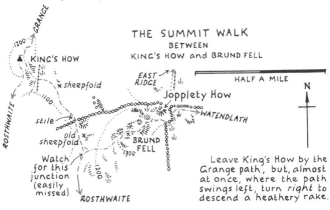

THE SUMMIT WALK
BETWEEN
KING'S HOW and BRUND FELL

GRANGE

1200

▲ KING'S HOW

ROSTHWAITE

1100

× sheepfold

stile

old sheepfold

Watch for this junction (easily missed)

ROSTHWAITE

EAST RIDGE

Joppletty How

WATENDLATH

BRUND FELL

1300

1200

HALF A MILE

N

Leave King's How by the Grange path, but, almost at once, where the path swings left, turn right to descend a heathery rake.

THE VIEW

Principal Fells

The views from the two main summits are very much alike, that from Brund Fell being a little more extensive but not so beautiful as that from King's How, the latter benefitting by a closer proximity to Borrowdale.

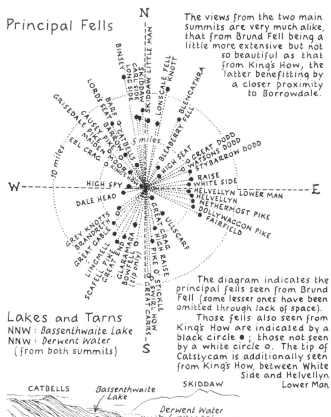

The diagram indicates the principal fells seen from Brund Fell (some lesser ones have been omitted through lack of space).

Those fells also seen from King's How are indicated by a black circle ● ; those not seen by a white circle ○. The tip of Catstycam is additionally seen from King's How, between White Side and Helvellyn Lower Man

Lakes and Tarns
NNW : *Bassenthwaite Lake*
NNW : *Derwent Water*
(from both summits)

looking north from the top of Brund Fell

78

The north ridge of King's How
with Skiddaw in the background

Borrowdale, from the lower slopes of Brund Fell

7 Barrow
from Braithwaite

The village of Braithwaite, a couple of miles west of Keswick, makes a very good base for a Lake District holiday. It has enough facilities and outdoor activities to keep families well occupied, with lots of superb fells and low-level walks within easy reach and the outdoor adventure centre of Whinlatter Forest a few miles away. But Braithwaite gets far fewer visitors than Keswick, which can sometimes feel over-run in summer, and makes for a relaxing alternative.

Barrow is Braithwaite's own personal fell, its distinctive rounded top looming protectively over the village to provide a popular stroll for locals and an ideal place from which to survey the village and its surroundings. Like many others in this part of the Lake District it has also been very much a working fell, mined for its lead between the seventeenth and late-nineteenth centuries. Its slopes carry the scars of the intense bursts of activity, with spoil heaps and mine openings on some of the slopes. Mining helped to build up Braithwaite into a substantial industrial community that was home to miners, millers, wool workers and a factory of the Cumberland Pencil Company – big enough to have a railway station of its own along the Cockermouth, Keswick and Penrith Railway, though this closed along with many other small lines in Cumbria in the 1960s.

This walk up Barrow follows Wainwright's suggested round journey from Braithwaite, with a climb that his notes describe as 'a favourite Sunday afternoon ramble . . . every step of the way is a joy'. As he points out, the uninterrupted views from the top are out of all proportion to the height, with views over two lakes and, on a good day, dozens of fells – 'A scene as fair as any in the kingdom.' Since the way up follows the spine of Barrow, with no obstructions to either side, there are good views all the way up from the village.

But the walk also provides young walkers with a good challenge, since the way up is a fairly steady slog, with few breaks from the steep gradient. The top is soon reached, but this is a good walk on which to get children used to the puff of Lake District walking. For those wanting a gentler ascent the route can be reversed, but bear in mind that this way around the steep side will have to be tackled coming down, which some walkers tend to find even harder. To extend the walk, turn left instead of right at Barrow Door on the way down, and follow the good path as far as you like towards Outerside, the parent fell of Barrow, and on to Sail.

From *Book Six: The North Western Fells*

Distance 3 miles (4.8km)

Ascent 1,250 feet (380m)

Start and finish point The car park at Braithwaite school (NY 233 237)

Ordnance Survey maps Explorer OL4; Landranger 89 or 90

Getting there

The car park at Braithwaite school is open to the public at weekends and in school holidays, and is a convenient place to start the walk. Put a donation for parking in the honesty box by the school. At other times, there is plenty of roadside parking around the village. To reach Braithwaite, follow the A66 west out of Keswick and look for the left turn soon after Portinscale (do not take the first turn to the village to the right). From further west and Cockermouth, the village can be reached over the B5289 – the Whinlatter Pass.

Braithwaite is served by the X5 bus, which connects to Keswick every hour from Mondays to Saturdays and every two hours on Sundays. The bus runs from Penrith to Workington – which both have train stations – with stops between including Rheged, Troutbeck, Threlkeld, Embleton and Cockermouth. From early April to early November, Braithwaite can also be reached on the 77 bus, the service that follows a circular route from Keswick to popular destinations including Portinscale, Catbells, Seatoller, Buttermere, Lorton and Whinlatter, four times a day daily.

Facilities, food and drink

Braithwaite has an excellent shop that sells picnic supplies including sandwiches and homemade cakes (017687 78088, www.braithwaitegeneralstore.co.uk). It is open daily and has lots of old-fashioned tubs of sweets that are useful for motivating children on the walk. It is passed soon after the start of the walk if you want to stock up on the way.

The village has good places to eat including The Royal Oak, likewise passed at the start of the walk (017687 78533, www. royaloak-braithwaite.co.uk), plus the Middle Ruddings Hotel (017687 78436, www.middle-ruddings.co.uk) and, just above it, the Coledale Inn (017687 78272, www.coledale-inn.co.uk). All have rooms to stay, and Braithwaite has a campsite, caravan park and B&Bs too.

There are plenty more walks from the village, including to the interesting attraction of Force Crag Mine, which was the Lake District's last working metal mine until it closed in 1990. It is spectacularly located in the Coledale valley and is now looked after by the National Trust, which opens it up to public tours a few days a year; check in advance for details (017687 74649, www.nationaltrust.org.uk). For more outdoor activities for children, a short drive west along the B5292 is Whinlatter Forest and its Visitor Centre, with walking and cycling trails, a zip wire adventure zone, playground and café (017687 78469, www. visitlakelandforests.co.uk). Keswick, with many more visitor attractions and places to eat and drink, is two miles to the east.

Directions

1 Turn left out of the school car park, soon passing the church. In front of The Royal Oak pub turn right and then, at the far

end of the pub, cross to turn left. The road passes between houses, then over a bridge and past a shop. About 80m on from the shop, where the road bends left, leave it to the right on a narrow road over a cattle-grid, signposted for Braithwaite Lodge. The ridge of Barrow and your way up it is now clearly visible to your half right. The road climbs, turns into a track, and then curves to the right of the farm buildings to cross a yard to a wooden gate (NY 233 232).

2 Cross through the gate and continue up, the way signposted for Newlands, to another, smaller wooden gate. Through this turn left. After just under 100m, by a small wooden post that indicates the way to Barrow, turn right up the grassy slope. It is a steady climb up from here, the way completely obvious and reinforced with steps ground into the grass by thousands of pairs of walking boots over the years. Don't forget to look back for views, including of Bassenthwaite Lake and Derwent Water. About halfway up, the path descends slightly to a flatter area with some remnants of old mining activity; this is a good place to catch your breath. The path then climbs again fairly relentlessly to the summit of Barrow (NY 227 218).

3 Continue on over the summit, soon dropping down and reaching Barrow Door, a junction of clear paths that is visible from the top (NY 222 217). Turn right here. The track drops steeply and pleasantly down, in parallel with Barrow on your right and Barrow Gill in the valley between. Further down the track gives way to broad, grassy slopes that are great for children to run down. It then becomes a track again, passing an underground reservoir, and reaches a gate that gives access to a paved road (NY 229 232). Follow this down back to Braithwaite. Just before the village proper there is a footpath branching off to the half right that cuts off a stretch of road; follow this down and bend to the right to emerge by the shop. Turn left, second right and left to return to the school car park.

Barrow

1494'

from Outerside
Stile End in the middle
distance; Stonycroft Gill
mine road down on the right

Braithwaite
●
GRISEDALE
▲ PIKE
OUTERSIDE   ▲ BARROW
▲   ●Stair
CAUSEY PIKE

MILES

0   1   2   3

from
Newlands Beck

NATURAL FEATURES

Barrow occupies an enviable position overlooking a scene as fair as any in the kingdom. In shape a long narrow ridge, rooted in Braithwaite, it rises to present a broad flank to the valley of Newlands before curving west, bounded by Stonycroft Gill, to join the mass of Outerside across the gap of Barrow Door. A great scar on the Newlands face marks the site of the once-famous Barrow Mine; on the opposite flank facing Coledale is another great scar, this one a natural formation, at a point where Barrow Gill, after an uneventful meandering from Barrow Door, is suddenly engulfed in a remarkable ravine, a gorge of amazing proportions for so slender a stream and deeper even than Piers Gill, which continues down, becoming wooded, to the cottages of Braithwaite. Bracken clothes the lower slopes of Barrow, but a dark cap of heather covers the higher reaches.

At Stonycroft Bridge an old water-cut (now dry) can be traced up, first carved in the rock and then following the contour of the fellside, with the gorge steeply below. The old level illustrated, half-hidden by gorse, is alongside the cut in its top part. This is the setting of the old Stonycroft Mine

Under Stonycroft Bridge. The beck enters the picture from the left. The dry watercut comes down on the right.

Barrow is 'the shivering mountain' of Lakeland. The great fan of spoil from the old mines on the Newlands face sweeps down to the road near Uzzicar and is prevented from burying it in debris only by a retaining parapet with a cleared space behind to accommodate major falls. The spoil is a sandy gravel constantly in slight motion, and the rustle of movement on the slope (no more than a whisper) can be heard on the road below. Note also an air shaft in the small field south of Uzzicar.

Barrow Gill

looking up
the gill to
Barrow Door
and
Causey Pike

looking down
the gill to
Braithwaite

MAP

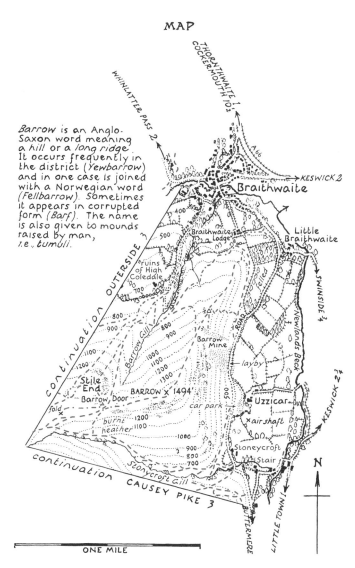

Barrow is an Anglo-Saxon word meaning a *hill* or a *long ridge*. It occurs frequently in the district (*Yewbarrow*) and in one case is joined with a Norwegian word (*Fellbarrow*). Sometimes it appears in corrupted form (*Barf*). The name is also given to mounds raised by man, i.e., *tumuli*.

ONE MILE

ASCENT FROM BRAITHWAITE
1250 feet of ascent : 1½ miles

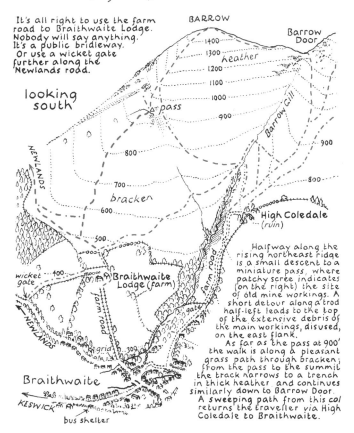

It's all right to use the farm road to Braithwaite Lodge. Nobody will say anything. It's a public bridleway. Or use a wicket gate further along the Newlands road.

looking south

BARROW

Barrow Door

1400
1300
1200
1100
1000
900

heather

Barrow Gill

pass

900

800

800

NEWLANDS

700

bracken

600

High Coledale
(ruin)

500

Halfway along the rising northeast ridge is a small descent to a miniature pass, where patchy scree indicates (on the right) the site of old mine workings. A short detour along a trod half-left leads to the top of the extensive debris of the main workings, disused, on the east flank.

wicket gate

400

Braithwaite Lodge (farm)

farm road

gate

As far as the pass at 900' the walk is along a pleasant grass path through bracken; from the pass to the summit the track narrows to a trench in thick heather and continues similarly down to Barrow Door. A sweeping path from this col returns the traveller via High Coledale to Braithwaite.

NEWLANDS

farm road

grid

300

Braithwaite

KESWICK

bus shelter

The ascent of Barrow from Braithwaite by its facing ridge is a favourite Sunday afternoon ramble, in the category of Latrigg and Catbells and Loughrigg Fell, and every step of the way is a joy. The walk can be extended, as indicated, to make a round journey of about two hours.

ASCENT FROM STAIR
1200 feet of ascent : 2¼ miles

looking north·west

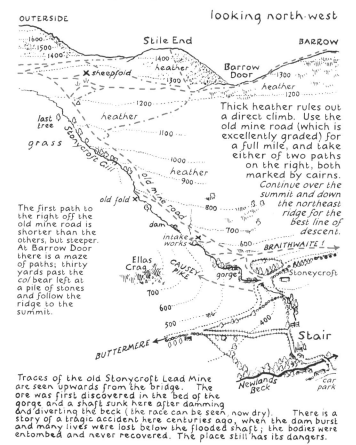

OUTERSIDE

1600 1500 1400

Stile End

1400 heather 1300

BARROW

Barrow Door 1300

heather 1200

✗ sheepfold

1200

last tree

heather

grass

Stonycroft Gill

1100

1000

heather 900

old fold ✗

old mine road

800

dam

700

intake works ✗

600

BRAITHWAITE !

Ellas Crag

CAUSEY PIKE

gorge

Stoneycroft

700

600

500

400

Stair

BUTTERMERE

Newlands Beck

car park

Thick heather rules out a direct climb. Use the old mine road (which is excellently graded) for a full mile, and take either of two paths on the right, both marked by cairns. *Continue over the summit and down the northeast ridge for the best line of descent.*

The first path to the right off the old mine road is shorter than the others, but steeper. At Barrow Door there is a maze of paths; thirty yards past the *col* bear left at a pile of stones and follow the ridge to the summit.

Traces of the old Stonycroft Lead Mine are seen upwards from the bridge. The ore was first discovered in the bed of the gorge and a shaft sunk here after damming and diverting the beck (the race can be seen, now dry). There is a story of a tragic accident here centuries ago, when the dam burst and many lives were lost below the flooded shaft; the bodies were entombed and never recovered. The place still has its dangers.

The old mine road has become a first-class walkers way into the hills, progress being fast and easy, and it lends itself well, coupled with a linking path from Braithwaite, to an ascent of Barrow, while giving an introduction to the quiet upper reaches of Stonycroft Gill. Causey Pike on the left of the valley dominates the walk throughout.

89

THE SUMMIT

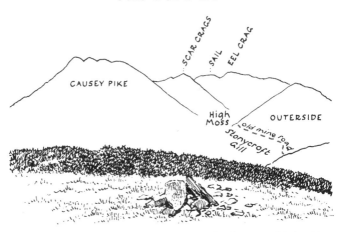

The highest point is situated on a patch of grass with heather all around. There is no cairn. On the right sort of day this is a grand place for settling down and getting the old pipe out for an hour's quiet meditation.

DESCENTS : Use only the track along the ridge, either way. In particular do not attempt a direct route for Newlands.

RIDGE ROUTE

To OUTERSIDE, 1863': 1¼ miles : WSW, then NW and SW

Depressions at 1270' and 1380'
800 feet of ascent
Rough walking in heather

Go down to Barrow Door and up a facing track, which gradually fades away. At the top of Stile End turn left down to Low Moss, across which a charming track mounts through the heather to the top of Outerside.

Not recommended beyond Barrow Door in mist.

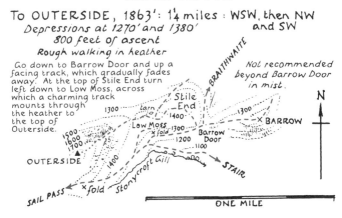

THE VIEW

This is a splendid panorama, too good really for the small effort involved in earning it.

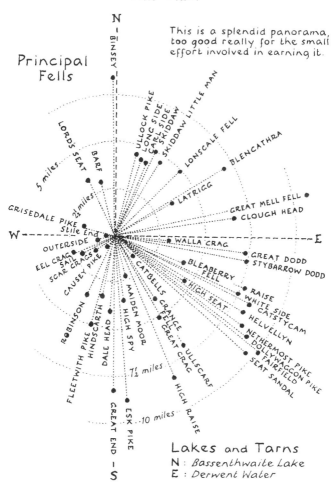

Principal Fells

Lakes and Tarns
N : Bassenthwaite Lake
E : Derwent Water

There is a remarkable contrast between the smiling Vale of Keswick, where Derwent Water is excellently displayed, and the sombre ring of fells crowded nearby in the west. Away over the head of Newlands is Esk Hause with Esk Pike soaring magnificently to the left of it and looking every inch a mountain

8 Dodd
from the Old Sawmill Tearoom

Unlike most of the fells recorded by Wainwright in his *Pictorial Guides*, Dodd has changed considerably since his day. No longer 'clothed from tip to toe' in trees, broad swathes of it have been cut down by the Forestry Commission and will, in time, revert to the heather moorland that originally decorated it. The summit in particular is now totally different to the one Wainwright would have seen, with substantial felling making for much better views over Bassenthwaite Lake and a host of northern Lake District fells.

The clearing of Dodd has made it more accessible to the public, but these days it is more likely to be visited by bird watchers than walkers. That is because the area around Bassenthwaite Lake has, in the summers since 2001, been home to ospreys. After nest platforms were built in the woods to accommodate them, the birds have returned every year to raise chicks, and a partnership between the Forestry Commission, Lake District National Park Authortiy and the RSPB now works to foster their colonisation and give people the opportunity to watch them. For so long as the ospreys return to the area, the trio of organisations run an excellent viewing platform from the lower slopes of Dodd, usually opening on the birds' return from Africa in April and closing when they depart in the autumn. Chicks usually hatch in May or June.

The Osprey Project is very popular with children and families, but not many of them go on to climb Dodd. This is a shame, as the fell is a lovely and straightforward climb, more so since the tree clearances opened up a panorama from the top that on a clear day extends up to Scotland. The peaceful quiet of the upper slopes contrasts with the hive of activity further down, while the tree cover that remains on Dodd makes a nice change from the exposed fells elsewhere in the northern Lake District.

This route follows Wainwright's ascent from the Old Sawmill Tearoom at Dodd Wood car park, which makes an ideal base for the fell, viewing platform and the third attraction of Mirehouse.

Wayfinding needs a little care as forest paths can be confusing, and the wood is now rather different to the one shown on some Ordnance Survey maps. But as the route broadly follows the Forestry Commission's own trail to the summit of Dodd, green-tipped posts help to keep you on the right track throughout.

From *Book Five: The Northern Fells*

Distance 3 miles (4.8km)

Ascent 1,300 feet (400m)

Start and finish point The Old Sawmill Tearoom and pay-and-display car park at the edge of Dodd Wood (NY 235 282)

Ordnance Survey maps Explorer OL4; Landranger 89 or 90

Getting there

The Old Sawmill Tearoom is attached to the main pay-and-display car park for Dodd Wood, just off the A591 at the south eastern corner of Bassenthwaite Lake. From Keswick, follow the A591 north for about 4 miles, then look for the car park on the right; it is also indicated as the place to park for Mirehouse. There is alternative, free parking on lay-bys along the A591.

The car park has a bus stop right outside, making this walk ideal for a trip out from Keswick. Take the 554 bus towards Carlisle, and ask for the Mirehouse stop. The starting point is also served by the 73 bus – the Caldbeck Rambler – that runs between Keswick and Carlisle with stops at popular places and including Castlerigg, Threlkeld, Hesket Newmarket, Caldbeck and Bassenthwaite village. It runs a few times a day from April to November, and on Saturdays only in the winter.

Facilities, food and drink

There is enough to do in and around Dodd Wood to turn this walk into a day's outing. The Old Sawmill Tearoom serves good lunches as well as tea and cakes, and makes an excellent end to the walk (017687 74317, www.theoldsawmill.co.uk; it closes on Wednesdays, and from late November to mid-February). You can stock up here with drinks and snacks for the walk. Public toilets are next door to the tearoom.

The osprey viewing points provide plenty for children to do, though it is worth checking in advance to see if the ospreys are *in situ* (017687 78469, www.ospreywatch.co.uk). For those who want to see more, there is another viewing platform further up Dodd; ask staff for directions. An exhibition about the ospreys is housed at the Whinlatter Visitor Centre to the south west, which has adventure playgrounds and a Go Ape course among other attractions (017687 78469, www.visitlakelandforests.co.uk).

A short walk across the road from the car park – cross with care – is Mirehouse, a fine old house with lots of connections to the Lake District's rich literary history (017687 72287, www.mirehouse.com). Wordsworth, Tennyson, Carlyle and many others stayed here, and there are collections of manuscripts and portraits; perhaps more importantly for children, there are also very good adventure playgrounds. The house is still lived in and is open only on Wednesday and Sunday afternoons (plus Fridays in August), though the gardens and playgrounds are open every day from early April to late October. Tickets can be bought at the Old Sawmill Tearoom.

Walkers with energy left after Dodd might like to explore some of the other trails through the wood; maps are available from the tearoom. Another very worthwhile stroll is the path down from Mirehouse to St Bega's Church, a beautiful and peaceful church perched idyllically beside Bassenthwaite Lake that dates back to around 950 (www.stbega.org.uk).

Directions

1 From the car park, walk towards the two buildings – the Old Sawmill Tearoom and the public toilets – and cut between them up to a wooden footbridge. Bear right in the direction of the signpost. The very clear path rises up the wooded fellside, at first with Skill Beck to your left, then bends sharply away from it to the right. About 80m after it does so, meet a junction of paths. For the osprey viewing platform, turn right and continue a short distance to the clearing. Otherwise turn left up the hillside. (From the viewing point, return to this junction and head up, the junction on your right from this direction.)

2 This track rises steadily up among the trees to a T-junction with another track. Turn left along it. About 100m further on it meets another junction; here bend right on a virtual hairpin. The path curves flat around the hillside at first, then starts to climb again, soon revealing the end of Bassenthwaite Lake to your right. Very soon after it does so, turn off the path to your left, marked by a green-tipped post. Climb fairly gently through the trees, and at a clearing and crossroads with an overgrown forest track continue ahead, again following the green post. Further up, as the trees thin out, there is a short diversion to the right for a viewpoint (NY 247 271). Back on the path, very soon reach a T-junction. Turn left along this for a final burst of climbing to the summit of Dodd, marked by a fine obelisk (NY 244 273). Walk on a little way west for more fine views of the lake.

3 Retrace your steps back down from the summit to the last T-junction. Turn left here to descend, soon picking up shelter from trees, and then making a hairpin bend to the left. This drops down to a broader track on the col (NY 249 274). Bear left along it and, about 70m on at a fork, left again. The way back down is now clear, with canopies of trees and the sound of Skill Beck in the valley to your right. Ignore all side-paths to your left to stay close to the beck, then reach a crossroads of paths. This is the junction for the osprey viewing platform reached earlier; turn right for the car park.

Dodd

also variously known
as Skiddaw Dodd
and Little Dodd
and named Dodd Fell
on Bartholomews maps

from Longside Wood

from
Millbeck
road end

- Bassenthwaite

▲ SKIDDAW

▲ CARL SIDE

▲ DODD

- Dancing Gate
- Millbeck

Little
Crosthwaite

Keswick ●

MILES

0   1   2   3

96

NATURAL FEATURES

Dodd, like Latrigg, can be described as a whelp of Skiddaw crouched at the feet of his parent. But Dodd has latterly shown nothing of the family characteristics and the old man must today regard his offspring with surprise and growing doubt, and feel like denying his paternity and disowning the little wretch.

Skiddaw is a high, bare, rangy mountain, open to the winds of heaven; Dodd is stunted, and (apart from a few areas that have recently been cleared) is clothed from tip to toe in a growth of trees so luxurious that scarcely any part of the original appearance of the fell remains in view. Skiddaw is Lakeland through and through, one of the respected dignitaries of the district, absolutely true blue; Dodd would seem more in place in the dense and steaming jungles of the Amazon.

But Dodd is really an innocent party in this matter, the great change being none of his seeking but having been thrust upon him. In years gone by Dodd sported a few small woodlands, like a young man his first moustaches, with such success and evidence of fertility as to attract the attention of the Forestry Commission, then developing the Thornthwaite Forest just across Bassenthwaite Lake. Since 1920 the Commission have been rampant here, and, except for a single field at Little Crosthwaite, they have covered the fell thickly with growing timber.

The work has been tackled with imagination, and with due regard to amenity. Nobody is likely to complain much about the results of this enterprise. There might be a little regret that the regimentation and segregation of species is still persisted in, giving an unnatural patchwork effect, but, in general, Dodd has come through the transformation fairly well. The older deciduous trees fringing the base of the fell have been retained as a screen, and, where they occur elsewhere, have been left to develop; many of the matured pines and firs in the early plantations, growing singly, are excellent specimens, and there has been a fair mixing of species in the new plantations, with larch, spruce, pine and fir in variety.   Admirable roads have been made, to give access to all parts of the forest, and it requires only a walk along them to appreciate the extent of the work involved in the maintenance of a great industry of this sort, and the skill and resource of those responsible for the enterprise. Dodd has not been spoiled, but given a new look; and it is a more

Scots pine

continued

Larch

NATURAL FEATURES

continued

interesting, and certainly a more fascinating, place than ever it was in the past. Skiddaw's frown betrays an old prejudice; true, Skiddaw has long had his own Forest but *that* is fine rolling upland country not desecrated by fancy trees..... *foreign* trees, moreover! If there *must* be trees on Dodd, aren't Lakeland trees good enough? Bah! says Skiddaw.

Douglas fir

Sitka spruce

As far as walkers are concerned, they may walk along the forest roads — *but not as of right*, and the courtesy thus extended is one that ought to be fully respected, please.

Only if it is desired to visit the summit of the fell is it necessary to leave the roads, and that objective can be reached, without causing damage to trees, using the path laid out in 2002 to the summit from the south-east. There is no excuse at all for barging through the plantations and crippling young trees.

The Forestry Commission refer to their plantations in this area by the title of Dodd Wood, and, because for many years the fell was completely covered, Dodd and Dodd Wood are often used as synonymous names; not always correctly, for the adjoining plantations on Long Side and north to Ravenstone are also part of the official Dodd Wood.

Geographically, Dodd is the first of the three great steps of Skiddaw rising from the head of Bassenthwaite Lake. The second step, Carl Side, is joined at mid-height: the link is a distinctive col from which flow the boundary streams, Skill Beck and Scale Beck. A feature is the pronounced northwest ridge; a less conspicuous ridge descends southeast from the summit. These ridges used to be followed by a wide fire-break amongst the dense plantations, resembling, from a distance, a centre parting in a head of hair. Today, in any view in which it can be seen, Dodd is readily identifiable by the dark covering of conifers on its slopes and its bare summit.

In 2001 the Forestry Commission laid out a series of circular walks all starting and finishing at the Old Sawmill Tearoom:
1. The Sandbed Gill Trail (marked by yellow-topped posts)
2. The Skill Beck Trail (marked by red-topped posts)
3. The Douglas Fir Trail (marked by blue-topped posts)
4. The Dodd Summit Trail (marked by green-topped posts)
The length varies from 1 mile to 3 miles; a leaflet is available at the tea room.

MAP

When the map on this page was prepared in 1962 it was the best available to the public at the time. It was the result of an amateur survey, using jigsaw tactics in lieu of precise instruments, but was quite reliable. Now that the map has been revised using satellite technology it is possible that it is still the best available. The prominent zig-zag path that approaches the summit from the south-east is not shown on Harvey's map of 2006, and on the 2008 edition of the 2½" Ordnance Survey map it is shown but the wrong shape.

CASTLE INN 3

continuation LONG SIDE 3

continuation LONG SIDE 3

continuation CARL SIDE 3

ONE MILE

N

car park

Longside Wood

Skill Beck

Little Crosthwaite

Forest roads

DODD 1647'

Long Doors

col

stile

stile

Long Close

Scalebeck Gill

Dancing Gate

Lyzzick Hall

Oakfield House

MAIN ROAD

Millbeck

KESWICK 2

A: Car park and main entrance to Dodd Wood

FOREST BOUNDARY

MAIN ROAD

MAIN ROAD

On the map on the left forest roads are indicated by a line (———) and disused roads by a pecked line (— — —). All forest roads are unenclosed by fences. The small map also shows contours at 250' intervals.

Dodd Wood

The wide variety of tree species in Dodd Wood, unusual in coniferous plantations, adds an interest for observant visitors. The deciduous trees are old favourites, generally well-known; but there is difficulty to the untrained eye in identifying the softwood timber trees, which are of the same habit of growth and similar in appearance. All are evergreen, except the larch, and grow straight and tall from a main stem.

Of the species planted most extensively, the pines and the larches are distinctive enough to be recognised at sight, but there is much doubt about the firs and the spruces.

Douglas Fir and Norway Spruce (the latter being the 'Christmas Tree') look very much alike, but can be identified with certainty by their cones, which litter the ground beneath the older trees. The cone of the Douglas Fir (next page) has peculiar three-pronged bracts issuing between the scales, but the cone of the Norway Spruce is smooth, the scales overlapping closely and appearing to be made of brown paper. Sitka Spruce is easier to distinguish by reason of its sturdy and vigorous growth, prickly needles and blue-green colour.

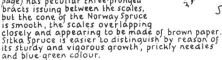

Scots Pine

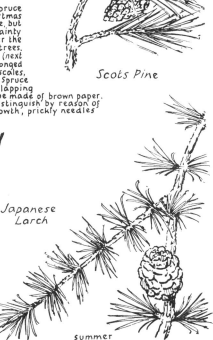

Japanese Larch

winter

summer

Dodd Wood

The Forestry Commission's publication "Thornthwaite"* mentions the following species as in cultivation on Dodd (apart from deciduous trees):

  Scots pine
  Lodgepole pine
  Mountain pine
  Norway spruce
  Sitka spruce
  Japanese larch
  European larch
  Douglas fir
  Noble fir
  Western hemlock
  Lawson's cypress
  Western red cedar

The four last-named are not much in evidence. Douglas Fir is extensive up to 1000'; larch occurs in big 'stands' at middle height, 800'-1200'; the spruces thrive, Sitka especially, up to 1500', and the pines at all elevations.

* *now out of print*

Douglas Fir

Norway Spruce

Sitka Spruce

ASCENTS

The climbing of Dodd is not to be achieved merely by repeating the process of putting one foot before and higher than the other, as in the case of most ascents. On Dodd the Forestry Commission and a million or so allies in a massed formation — spruces, firs and larch (to say nothing of *Pinus mugo*) — must be outwitted, and some crafty manoeuvring is required to reach the summit. Forcing a way ever upwards through the trees is not playing the game, and is out of the question anyway because the depths of the forest are quite impassable. Recourse must therefore be had to (a) the forest roads and (b) the forest paths.

THE FOREST ROADS:

The forest workers know not only how to grow trees but how to plan roads too, and they have made a really excellent job of laying passages for their vehicles. Considering the steepness of the fell the roads are wonderfully well graded, reaching to all parts of the forest without ever exceeding the gentlest of slopes, and they are well culverted, providing dry surfaces for walking even on the wettest days. Roughly metalled, they are not hard to the feet but are generally shaly, rather loose and soft. In long spirals and zigzags the roads climb as high as 1400 feet; some other means of access must be used, therefore, in later stages of the ascent to the summit, 200' higher.

Forest road

Dodd is a small fell, yet there are already nearly five miles of 10' roads hidden amongst the plantations. In the contiguous Longside Wood (under the same management) are several more miles of forest roads, similarly concealed from the sight of travellers on the busy Keswick-Carlisle highway running along the base of the plantations.

At two places, forest roads effect junctions with the main road. These may be used by walkers to enter the forest, but it is more usual to use the entrance by the Old Sawmill Tearoom, where there is a bus stop and car park. (From April to October the tea room car park is currently also used by visitors to Mirehouse, the historic home of the Spedding family, on the occasions when it is open to the public. Mirehouse is where Alfred Lord Tennyson was staying when he wrote *Morte d'Arthur*.)

ASCENTS

continued

THE FOREST PATHS :
Before the forest roads were cut the workers in the new plantations made use of a network of footpaths between the growing trees. Many of these old paths have gone out of

commission or been superseded by the roads; others can still be traced although now heavily overshadowed; a few remain in regular use. Since Dodd Wood became part of the Whinlatter Forest Park new paths have been constructed for the benefit of visitors. Consequently there is now a surfaced route all the way from the car park to the summit; if you want to climb a mountain but left your boots at home this is the place to come. According to O.S. maps many of the forest paths form part of long distance walks, particularly the Allerdale Ramble, which runs from Borrowdale to the coast.

Forest path

THE FOREST RIDES (FIRE-BREAKS) :
The fire-breaks were strips of rough fellside that were left unplanted to stop a fire spreading from one part of the forest to another. In 2006 no trace of any of them could be found.

THE DISUSED FOREST ROADS :
These are shown on the small map on page 4. They become overgrown with moss, heather and, eventually, young trees.

Fire-break
(north-west ridge)

THE FELLED AREAS :
Except in the area around the summit these are not shown on the maps. Felling is going on all the time, and if you look closely at felled areas you will often find that young trees have been planted or have naturally regenerated.

THE OSPREY VIEWING POINT :
This is shown on the diagram on page 9. It is open only from April to August because the birds migrate to Africa for the winter. Telescopes are provided for watching a nest on the far side of the lake. There are only two osprey breeding sites in England, the other being in Rutland. In 2008 the birds moved to Dodd Wood, and another viewing point was set up farther up the hill.

ASCENT FROM THE OLD SAWMILL TEAROOM
1300 feet of ascent : 2½ miles

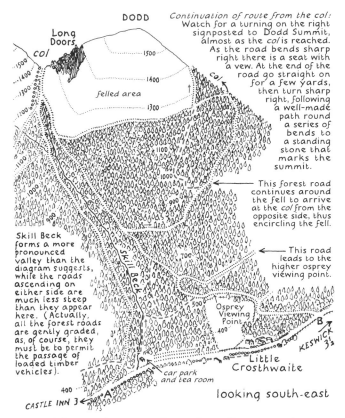

DODD

Long Doors

col

felled area

1500

1400

1300

1100

1000

900

800

700

600

500

Osprey Viewing Point

400

B

KESWICK 3½

Little Crosthwaite

car park and tea room

CASTLE INN 3

Skill Beck

looking south-east

Continuation of route from the col:
Watch for a turning on the right signposted to Dodd Summit, almost as the *col* is reached. As the road bends sharp right there is a seat with a view. At the end of the road go straight on for a few yards, then turn sharp right, following a well-made path round a series of bends to a standing stone that marks the summit.

— This forest road continues around the fell to arrive at the *col* from the opposite side, thus encircling the fell.

— This road leads to the higher osprey viewing point.

Skill Beck forms a more pronounced valley than the diagram suggests, while the roads ascending on either side are much less steep than they appear here. (Actually, all the forest roads are gently graded, as, of course, they must be to permit the passage of loaded timber vehicles).

A and B are the two points where forest roads come down to the public highway. Both roads lead directly to the Long Doors *col*: in fact, they converge below it. The *col* is an interesting place, with unexpected cliffs.

The route from the *col* onwards lies on the far side of the fell and is not shown in the diagram (see note at top of page). An alternative route, not visiting the *col*, and about the same length, follows the south side of Skill Beck from the tea room and is marked throughout its length by posts with a green band round them. It is indicated by arrows on the diagram. Both routes are thoroughly recommended.

ASCENT FROM DANCING GATE
1320 feet of ascent : 1½ miles

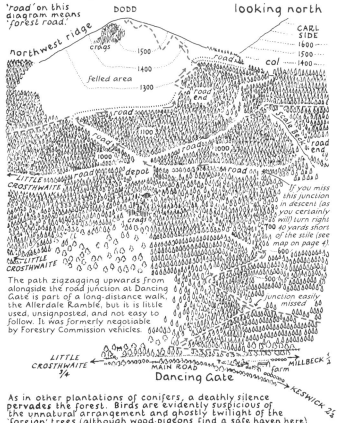

'road' on this diagram means 'forest road.'

looking north

As in other plantations of conifers, a deathly silence pervades the forest. Birds are evidently suspicious of the unnatural arrangement and ghostly twilight of the 'foreign' trees (although wood-pigeons find a safe haven here) and prefer the friendlier atmosphere of deciduous woodlands, where the sun can reach them and they can be happy and sing.

This is more a game than a walk. Snakes-and-ladders enthusiasts will find the route absorbing. Apart from the felled areas near the summit Dodd is a labyrinth of forest roads and paths. These are all the more confusing because the dense screen of trees makes it impossible to view the way ahead or to take bearings. Follow the arrows.

ASCENT FROM MILLBECK
1250 feet of ascent : 2 miles

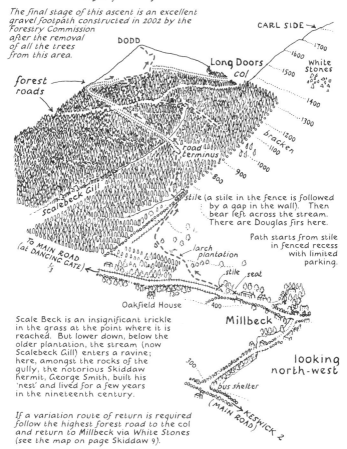

The final stage of this ascent is an excellent gravel footpath constructed in 2002 by the Forestry Commission after the removal of all the trees from this area.

DODD

CARL SIDE

Long Doors col

White Stones

1700
1600
1500
1400
1300
1200
bracken
1100
1000
900
800

forest roads

road terminus

Scalebeck Gill

stile (a stile in the fence is followed by a gap in the wall). Then bear left across the stream. There are Douglas firs here.

Path starts from stile in fenced recess with limited parking.

TO MAIN ROAD (at DANCING GATE) 1/3

larch plantation

stile   seat

Oakfield House   400

Millbeck

looking north-west

300

bus shelter

KESWICK 2 (MAIN ROAD)

Scale Beck is an insignificant trickle in the grass at the point where it is reached. But lower down, below the older plantation, the stream (now Scalebeck Gill) enters a ravine; here, amongst the rocks of the gully, the notorious Skiddaw hermit, George Smith, built his 'nest' and lived for a few years in the nineteenth century.

If a variation route of return is required follow the highest forest road to the col and return to Millbeck via White Stones (see the map on page Skiddaw 9).

Millbeck is conveniently placed for an ascent of Dodd, yet this is not a popular climb, and nobody will be encountered (except on the final stage) on 360 days in the year. The route up Scalebeck Gill is impracticable, and the forest is a maze, but follow the arrows and the top will be reached in due course.

THE SUMMIT

Anyone visiting the summit today would not recognise the drawing above: all the trees have gone, and the cairn has been replaced by a standing stone which bears the inscription 'Dodd Summit 1612 feet'. Presumably the stone was erected before the altitude was reassessed by the Ordnance Survey as 502 metres or 1647 feet. On the reverse of the stone are memorials to John Lole and Ian Sandelands of the first Seaton Scout Group, and to Malcolm McDougall. The trees were mountain pines, *Pinus mugo*. They covered the top completely, except for a tiny clearing which was left in deference to the cairn. Fifty years ago it was noted that the planting did not appear to be successful. Few trees were then flourishing: the majority looked unhealthy or even diseased and dying. The trees have not completely disappeared, for their stumps still remain, and the ground is littered with dead branches, which make walking difficult.

The path to the summit from the east was built in 2002.

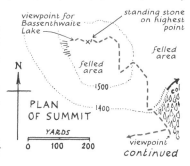

PLAN
OF SUMMIT

viewpoint for
Bassenthwaite
Lake

standing stone
on highest
point

felled
area

felled
area

1500

1400

viewpoint
continued

N

YARDS
0   100   200

˙˙˙˙˙˙˙ forest road
- - - - - path leading to
forest road

THE SUMMIT

continued

DESCENTS : The path to the west (towards Bassenthwaite Lake) soon comes to an end, and all descents start along the path to the east. When you come to a forest road there is a choice of routes. For the tea room stay on the road to the *col* and follow the valley of Skill Beck, or go left and immediately right at the start of the forest road and follow the green-topped posts. For Millbeck go left and immediately right at the start of the forest road, following the ridge. Then take a path on the right, which later becomes a forest road and bends sharp left. When you get to the main forest road turn right and immediately left onto a lesser road. After crossing Scalebeck Gill this becomes a path, which eventually leads to Millbeck. For Dancing Gate use the Millbeck route and turn right forty yards before leaving the plantation. The zigzag path to Dancing Gate is impossible to find from above.

RIDGE ROUTE

To CARL SIDE, 2447': 1½ miles :
    SE, then NE and N
    Depression at 1355'
    1075 feet of ascent
    An interesting traverse.
Follow the path down to the forest road and turn left to the *col.* Turn right for a hundred yards, and then left, crossing the forest fence by a stile. From the stile a path rises obliquely through the heather and comes out at the south ridge of Carl Side just above the main rash of White Stones. The ridge is then followed up.

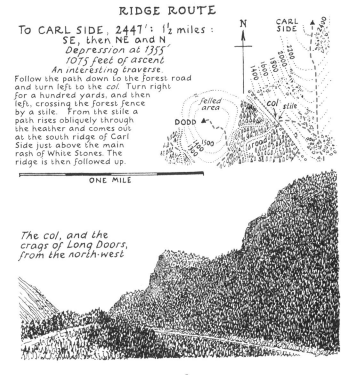

The col, and the crags of Long Doors, from the north-west

THE VIEW

When trees covered the summit one could not see all the fells indicated on the diagram below without standing on tiptoes, craning the neck, leaping in the air and miscellaneous gyrations of the body not normally indulged in by people in their right senses. The felling has transformed the prospect. Only parts of Bassenthwaite Lake can be seen from the summit, but the whole of the lake can be seen by continuing beyond the summit to the end of the gravel path. In 1993 the area around the lake became a National Nature Reserve.

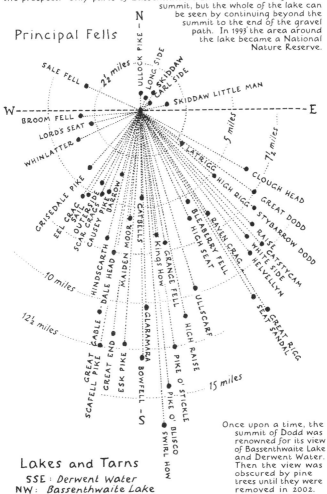

Principal Fells

Once upon a time, the summit of Dodd was renowned for its view of Bassenthwaite Lake and Derwent Water. Then the view was obscured by pine trees until they were removed in 2002.

Lakes and Tarns
SSE: Derwent Water
NW: Bassenthwaite Lake

9 Castle Crag
from Rosthwaite

Castle Crag has been a first Lake District fell for generations of young walkers. A short enough climb to be manageable for even small children, yet high and dramatic enough for a sense of accomplishment and good views, it is an ideal half-day excursion for families. Or as Wainwright puts it in his notes: 'If a visitor to Lakeland has only two to three hours to spare, poor fellow, yet desperately wants to reach a summit and take back an enduring memory of the beauty and atmosphere of the district . . . let him climb Castle Crag.'

At less than 1,000 feet, this is the lowest of the 214 fells covered in Wainwright's seven *Pictorial Guides*, and some walkers do not consider it a 'proper' summit, but a small extension of High Spy. But as he points out, it makes up for its lack of stature in plenty of other ways, and fully deserves its status as a separate and 'magnificently independent' fell with a very distinctive peak. As well as being a fine climb in its own right, it is the perfect way to appreciate the beautiful area at the head of Borrowdale – to which Wainwright gave the considerable accolade of 'the loveliest square mile in Lakeland'.

This walk approaches Castle Crag from Rosthwaite, a pretty Borrowdale village with a hotel pub and tearooms, and returns along the River Derwent, which has excellent spots for picnics, stone skimming and paddling and, on warm days, is a good and popular place for swimming. Despite the modest height, the final stretch of climbing is not entirely straightforward, with a path through steep piles of slate left over from the mining that has taken large chunks out of Castle Crag over the years. Care is also needed on top of the fell as there are some sheer drops around. The walk can be shortened by nearly 1 mile by returning the way you came, though the alternative route back is worth the extra distance. It can be extended a little by following the Cumbria Way footpath on which you return to Rosthwaite, either north to Grange or south to Stonethwaite.

From *Book Six: The North Western Fells*

Distance 4 miles (6.4km)

Ascent 700 feet (215m)

Start and finish point The National Trust car park in Rosthwaite (NY 258 149)

Ordnance Survey maps Explorer OL4; Landranger 89 or 90

Getting there

Rosthwaite is on the B5289 south of Derwent Water. From Keswick, follow the signs for Borrowdale. The car park is on the right as you arrive in the village. It is free for National Trust members and can fill up quickly in the summer. If it is full there are more spaces by the Borrowdale Institute next door; put a contribution for parking here in the honesty box in the wall.

Rosthwaite can be reached from Keswick on the 78 bus, which runs every half an hour in the summer and every hour in other seasons and on Sundays. The buses are usually open top, which is a delight on warm days and a distinct negative on rainy ones. From the bus stop in Rosthwaite, continue walking in the same direction as the bus and take the first right up to the starting point.

From early April to early November, Rosthwaite is also served daily by the 77 bus, which runs on a circuit from Keswick to Buttermere, High Lorton and the Whinlatter Forest. For anyone wishing to put together a longer day's walking, the bus stops along the way include starting points for more walks in this book, including Catbells from near Hawse End by Derwent Water and Haystacks from Gatesgarth.

Facilities, food and drink

For refreshments before or after the walk, call in at the Flock-In tearooms, close to the starting point (017687 77675, www.borrowdaleherdwick.co.uk). As well as tea and cakes, it sells good lunches including stews and pasties made with local Herdwick lamb. Further on through the village is the Scafell Hotel, which has a public bar and good meals (017687 77208, www.scafell.co.uk).

Back towards Keswick, the village of Grange has two good cafés, while a short drive or walk further down the Borrowdale valley are the villages of Stonethwaite, which has a tiny and delightful tearoom and the Langstrath pub and hotel (017687 77239, www.thelangstrath.com); and Seatoller, just beyond which is the Honister Slate Mine, an interesting attraction high in the hills with mine tours, a via ferrata, shop and café (017687 77230, www.honister.com). It can be reached on the 77 bus from Rosthwaite, as can the visitor centre at Whinlatter Forest west of Keswick, which has children's adventure trails, a zip wire adventure zone and a café (017687 78469, www. visitlakelandforests.co.uk). Keswick itself has lots of shops, pubs, cafés and family-friendly attractions. Start a visit here at the Tourist Information Centre in the Moot Hall on Market Square (017687 72645).

Directions

1 Turn right out of the car park and up past buildings, including the Flock-In tearooms on your right. Beyond, bear right on to a farm track that passes farm buildings and barns on your left before being enclosed on both sides by a wall and hedgerow. It leads up to a river; cross this immediately via the easy stepping stones or, if children are reluctant, continue along the river bank for 150m and cross it over a lovely old stone bridge instead. If crossing the stones, turn right immediately after through a small wooden gate, and follow the path up to the stone bridge. Continue on the clear track up to two large wooden gates, and take the right-hand

one to continue along the river. Castle Crag is in view to your half left here. Just over 200m on, the track forks; bear left to curve away from the river. Just over 100m further, it passes a large wooden gate and stile to the left (NY 252 155). Leave the track through this gate to bear left up the grassy slopes.

2 The path climbs steeply, soon over a flight of stone steps and under cover of trees, to a small wooden gate in a wall. Beyond, another flight of steps leads up to a flat grassy area. Continue over this, the path bearing slightly right, to a ladder stile in another wall. Over it the path goes right and then zig-zags up amid huge piles of slate; take care with small children here. At the top of the zig-zags, bear right for a short final climb up to the summit of Castle Crag, marked by a memorial stone to local men who died in the First World War, with a cairn on top (NY 249 159). As Castle Crag's name suggests, this summit area was probably once home to an ancient hill fort.

3 Retrace your steps to the bottom of the slate zig-zags, taking care as you drop. For an alternative way back to Rosthwaite, turn right to drop again, down to a fence. Turn right and almost immediately cross the fence to your left by a stile then a ladder stile. Drop down beyond to pass through a gap in a wall and on to a clear path that runs across you. Turn right along it. Castle Crag rises steeply up to your right. The very obvious path drops steadily, and after about 500m meets and crosses a small footbridge where it forks. Take the right-hand path by a wall, which descends towards the River Derwent. Just before the river, turn right along a path, signposted for Rosthwaite (NY 251 165). After just under ½ mile, follow the fork in the path that is again signposted for Rosthwaite. After 1 mile it returns to the bridge over the river reached earlier. Cross either here or via the stepping stones further on, and return down the track to Rosthwaite.

Castle Crag

951'

Grange
●

CASTLE
▲ CRAG

Rosthwaite
●

ONE MILE

from the south

NATURAL FEATURES

Perhaps, to be strictly correct, Castle Crag should be regarded not as a separate fell but as a protuberance on the rough breast of Low Scawdel, occurring almost at the foot of the slope and remote from the ultimate summit of High Spy far above and out of sight. Castle Crag has no major geographical function — it is not a watershed, does not persuade the streams of Scawdel from their predestined purpose of joining the Derwent and interrupts only slightly the natural fall of the fell to Borrowdale: on the general scale of the surrounding heights it is of little significance.

Yet Castle Crag is so magnificently independent, so ruggedly individual, so aggressively unashamed of its lack of inches, that less than justice would be done by relegating it to a paragraph in the High Spy chapter. Its top is below 1000 feet (its 'official' height in 2008 being 951 feet), which makes it the only fell below 1000 feet in this series of books that is awarded the 'full treatment', a distinction well earned.

Castle Crag conforms to no pattern. It is an obstruction in the throat of Borrowdale, confining passage therein to the width of a river and a road, hiding what lies beyond, defying cultivation. Its abrupt pyramid, richly wooded from base almost to summit but bare at the top, is a wild tangle of rough steep ground, a place of crags and scree and tumbled boulders, of quarry holes and spoil dumps, of confusion and disorder. But such is the artistry of nature, such is the mellowing influence of the passing years, that the scars of disarray and decay have been transformed in a romantic harmony, cloaked by a canopy of trees and a carpet of leaves. There are lovely copses of silver birch by the crystal-clear river, magnificent specimens of Scots pine higher up. Naked of trees, Castle Crag would be ugly; with them, it has a sylvan beauty unsurpassed, unique.

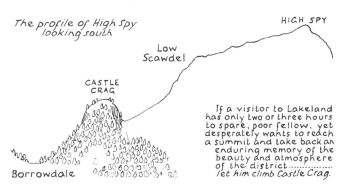

The profile of High Spy looking south

HIGH SPY

Low Scawdel

CASTLE CRAG

Borrowdale

If a visitor to Lakeland has only two or three hours to spare, poor fellow, yet desperately wants to reach a summit and take back an enduring memory of the beauty and atmosphere of the district..............
let him climb Castle Crag.

Castle Crag 3

The summit-quarry

The pedestrian path to the
top goes up the grass
on the right

summit

Quarries and caves of Castle Crag

In addition to the summit-quarry, which is open to the sky
and obvious to all who climb the fell, the steep flank above the
Derwent is pitted with cuttings and caverns and levels, every
hole having its tell-tale spoilheap, but the scars of this former
industrial activity are largely concealed by a screen of trees
and not generally noticed. Much of this flank is precipitous,
the ground everywhere is very rough, and the vertically-hewn
walls of naked stone are dangerous traps for novice explorers.

Of these quarries the best known
is High Hows, the debris of which is
passed on the riverside walk from
Grange to Rosthwaite. A detour up
the quarry road leads to a series of
caverns of special interest because
in one of them Millican Dalton,
a mountaineering adventurer
and a familiar character in the
district between the wars (died
1947, aged 80), furnished a home
for his summer residence, using
an adjacent cave at a higher
level (the 'Attic') as sleeping
quarters. *Note here his lettering
(though now difficult to read) cut
in the rock at the entrance —*
'Don't!! Waste words, jump to conclusions'

The Attic

Millican's Cave

MAP

The thick line forming a square has a special significance. It encloses one mile of country containing no high mountain, no lake, no famous crag, no tarn. But, in the author's humble submission, it encloses the loveliest square mile in Lakeland — the Jaws of Borrowdale.

Here are seven more lovely square miles:
The Stonethwaite valley
The head of Ullswater
Tilberthwaite to Brathay
Lodore-Ashness
Dovedale
Around Rydal Water
The Buttermere valley
(not in order of merit)

Map continuations:
to the west   HIGH SPY 4
to the south   DALE HEAD 4

117

ASCENT FROM GRANGE
CASTLE CRAG
700 feet of ascent
1½ miles

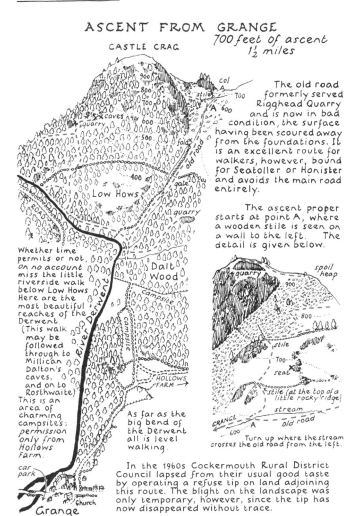

The old road formerly served Rigghead Quarry and is now in bad condition, the surface having been scoured away from the foundations. It is an excellent route for walkers, however, bound for Seatoller or Honister and avoids the main road entirely.

The ascent proper starts at point A, where a wooden stile is seen on a wall to the left. The detail is given below.

Whether time permits or not, on no account miss the little riverside walk below Low Hows Here are the most beautiful reaches of the Derwent. (This walk may be followed through to Millican Dalton's caves, and on to Rosthwaite) This is an area of charming campsites: permission only from Hollows Farm.

As far as the big bend of the Derwent all is level walking.

Turn up where the stream crosses the old road from the left.

In the 1960s Cockermouth Rural District Council lapsed from their usual good taste by operating a refuse tip on land adjoining this route. The blight on the landscape was only temporary, however, since the tip has now disappeared without trace.

Leave Grange by a lane (signposted to Hollows Farm) almost opposite the church.

ASCENT FROM ROSTHWAITE

700 feet of ascent
1¼ miles

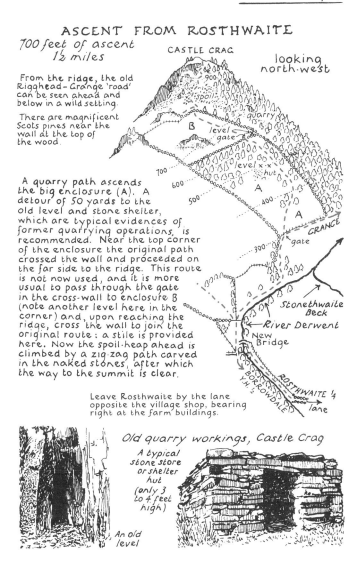

CASTLE CRAG

looking north-west

From the ridge, the old Rigghead–Grange 'road' can be seen ahead and below in a wild setting.

There are magnificent Scots pines near the wall at the top of the wood.

A quarry path ascends the big enclosure (A). A detour of 50 yards to the old level and stone shelter, which are typical evidences of former quarrying operations, is recommended. Near the top corner of the enclosure the original path crossed the wall and proceeded on the far side to the ridge. This route is not now used, and it is more usual to pass through the gate in the cross-wall to enclosure B (note another level here in the corner) and, upon reaching the ridge, cross the wall to join the original route: a stile is provided here. Now the spoil-heap ahead is climbed by a zig-zag path carved in the naked stones, after which the way to the summit is clear.

Leave Rosthwaite by the lane opposite the village shop, bearing right at the farm buildings.

Old quarry workings, Castle Crag

A typical stone store or shelter hut (only 3 to 4 feet high)

An old level

THE SUMMIT

The summit is circular in plan, about 60 yards in diameter, and a perfect natural stronghold. Even today, one man in possession, armed with a stick, could prevent its occupation by others whatever their number, there being one strategic point (the place of access to the top) where passage upward is restricted to single-file traffic. Authorities agree that there was once a fort here, probably early British, but it needs a trained eye to trace any earthworks—which, in any case, must have been severely disturbed by an old quarry that has cut a big slice out of the summit and, be it noted, constitutes an unprotected danger. Photographers (who have a habit of taking backward steps when composing their pictures) should take care lest they suddenly vanish.

The highest point is a boss of rock, and this is crowned by a low horseshoe-shaped wall, below which, set in the rock, is a commemorative tablet: a war memorial to the men of Borrowdale, effective and imaginative. Immediately to the west of the summit is a larch tree that blocks out much of High Spy, and other specimens surround the perimeter.

DESCENTS: For the ordinary walker there is only one way on and off, and this is on the south side, by a clump of larch, where a clear track descends between the edge of the quarry (right) and a cutting (left) to the flat top of the spoil-heap, at the end of which a ramp on the right inclines in zigzags to the grass below. Here, if bound for Rosthwaite, cross the wall on the left; for Grange the way continues down, crossing two walls by stiles, to the old Rigghead road.

ENVIRONS
OF THE SUMMIT

THE SUMMIT

When this guide was first published, the altitude of the summit (now officially 951 feet) had yet to be determined. It was frequently quoted as 900 feet, but the following reasoning demonstrated that it must actually be in excess of this figure.

From High Doat (927'; 1 mile south) the summit appears to be above the horizontal plane of Latrigg (1203'; 6½ miles), giving a height of not less than 970', and probably 980' or 990'.

Look at High Doat from Castle Crag: it is obviously lower.

THE VIEW

The view is circumscribed but is open to the north, where Derwent Water, backed by Skiddaw, makes a fine scene. The steep fall from the summit on all sides provides an aerial study of the beautiful detail of mid-Borrowdale.

Principal Fells

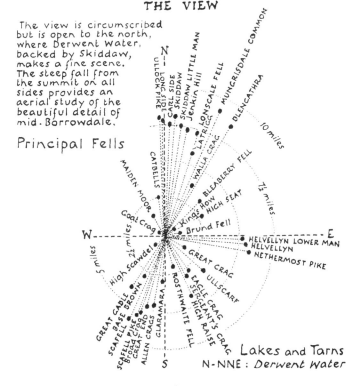

Lakes and Tarns
N-NNE: Derwent Water

10 Latrigg
from Keswick

Latrigg is Keswick's native fell and viewpoint – a much-loved regular stroll for locals and a common first Lake District fell for visitors. With easy walking throughout and a steadily gentle ascent, it is a place where small children can find their fellwalking feet.

Latrigg's broad shape is a distinctive sight from the town and beyond, and its slopes have been well trodden ever since the 1880s, when it was the subject of one of England's early mass trespasses in protest at landowners' refusal to open up access to walkers. The climbing by hundreds of people without permission eventually led to the opening of footpaths up Latrigg – including ones followed in this walk – and was a precursor to the more famous and influential mass trespass of Kinder Scout in 1932.

This walk follows Wainwright's suggested ascent of Latrigg from Keswick, soon leaving behind the busy town centre to pass through woods and up open fellside. Less than 1,000 feet of ascent is required to reach the top – only a handful of Lake District fells among the 214 described by Wainwright in his seven *Pictorial Guides* are lower in height than this – but with unobstructed views over Keswick, Derwent Water and many high fells beyond, few Lakeland fells provide such expansive panoramas at such modest altitude. Wainwright says of it in his notes: 'There is enough of interest in this charming picture to engage the attention for many hours, and Latrigg is a place to visit time and time again, for the scene is never quite the same but always fresh and exciting.' The grassy summit is a great place for children, with wide, safe spaces on which to play and picnic in the summer, though its exposed location means it is not a place to linger for long on cold or wet days.

An even easier way up Latrigg than this is to drive to the car park at the end of Gale Road, near Applethwaite to the north of the fell (NY 281 253). (The car park is a popular starting point for Skiddaw, usually considered the Lake District's fourth highest fell, and the parent of Latrigg.) From here it is a matter of minutes to the summit and a round trip of barely a mile. The route from here is even smoother than from Keswick, and the way along a specially made limited mobility path, clearly signposted all the way from the gates at the car park, can be managed with pushchairs and wheelchairs. But many children might find it too easy, and it does miss out on much of what Wainwright calls 'a very beautiful short walk'.

From *Book Five: The Northern Fells*

Distance 4½ miles (7.2km)

Ascent 950 feet (290m)

Start and finish point The Keswick Football Club car park off Crosthwaite Road in Keswick (NY 264 240)

Ordnance Survey maps Explorer OL4; Landranger 89 or 90

Getting there

The car park at the football club is the most convenient for this walk, and is reached by following the A5271 through Keswick. If you are arriving along the A66, take the turn-off near Crosthwaite on the western side of the town to save the drive through the centre, and look for the car park before you reach the T-junction. Put a donation in the car park's honesty box.

There are more car parks back in town, though they can fill up quickly. Street parking is limited by discs, and rigorously enforced by wardens. To reach the start of the walk from the centre of Keswick, head north west up Main Street, which becomes High Hill, with the River Greta soon on your right. Soon after the river bends away to the right, turn right on to Crosthwaite Road.

Keswick is very well served by buses, including the 555 from Kendal, Windermere and Ambleside; the 554 from Carlisle and Wigton; the X4 and X5 from Cockermouth and Penrith; the 77 from Buttermere; the 78 from Borrowdale; and the 208 from Penrith and Ullswater. The X4, X5 and 208 services also connect the walk up to the nearest train station at Penrith.

Facilities, food and drink

Keswick has lots of shops and cafés from which to make up a picnic for the walk, including branches of Booths (017687 73518, www.booths.co.uk); and the Co-op (017687 72688, www.co-operative.coop), on Main Street close to the start of the walk.

The town has lots of pubs and hotel bars, with the best including The Dog & Gun on Lake Road (017687 73463) and The Bank Tavern on Main Street (017687 75168). Cafés are numerous, and recommended ones include The Square Orange on St John's Street, with especially good pizzas (017687 73888, www.thesquareorange.co.uk); The Wild Strawberry on Main Street (017687 74399) and The Lakeland Pedlar wholefood café by the Bell Close car park (017687 74492, www.lakelandpedlar.co.uk. With no end of outdoor shops, Keswick is also a good place to stock up on family walking gear.

Family-friendly attractions in the town include the Pencil Museum, a short stroll back towards town from the start of the walk, and home to the world's first and longest pencils; it often has special events and displays for children (017687 73626, www.pencilmuseum.co.uk). On Museum Square is the Puzzling Place, dedicated to puzzles and optical illusions (017687 75102, www.puzzlingplace.co.uk). Fitz Park is a good place to head for too, home to a big children's playground and the Keswick Museum and Art Gallery and its displays on Lake District history and walking, plus quirky Victorian exhibits (017687 73263, www.keswickmuseum.webs.com). Just above the park is the town's swimming pool with a water slide (017687 72760, www.carlisleleisure.com). Other popular family activities include a ride on Derwent Water (017687 72263, www.keswick-launch.

co.uk). For more ideas for activities in and around Keswick, call into the Tourist Information Centre in the Moot Hall on Market Square (017687 72645); note the unusual one-handed clock on the hall's tower.

Directions

1 Turn right out of the car park up Crosthwaite Road, soon passing the hospital. Immediately after it, turn right on to Brundholme Road, and take the path through a wooden gate on your right to avoid the road. Where this runs out, rejoin the road as it passes houses. Past a right-hand turn for houses on Briar Rigg, turn off left on to Spoony Green Lane, with a public bridleway sign indicating Skiddaw. Soon the track crosses the busy A66, then reaches Spooney Green bed and breakfast (NY 270 244). Continue ahead on the broad track, passing an information board to your left. Ignoring all side-paths to your right, the path eventually reaches a viewpoint, Ewe How.

2 About 30m further on, at a junction of paths, take the left-hand one. It gradually rises, passing another information board on your left and picking up a fence on the same side. Where the track flattens out, look for a sharp turn on a path to the right, signposted for Latrigg. This broad path now zig-zags up the hillside, passing an old gatepost and, further on, a signpost indicating the Gate Road car park. Bear right here. The path now rises easily to a seat with fine views back over Keswick and beyond. Carry on a short distance to the flat, broad summit of Latrigg (NY 279 247).

3 Continue over the summit. Where the path meets a stile in a fence, bend sharp right along the fence and drop down to a stile that leads into the woods. Cross and descend along the path, which is covered by trees. It emerges at a forest track. Turn right. It pleasantly contours the southern side of Latrigg until it reaches the Ewe How viewpoint reached earlier. Turn left here to retrace your steps back along the track to the outskirts of Keswick.

Latrigg

1203'

This is the Latrigg near Keswick
— there is another,
less well-known,
near Over Water.

from the Blencathra Centre
(showing the east ridge going
down to Brundholme Woods)

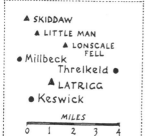

▲ SKIDDAW

  ▲ LITTLE MAN

    ▲ LONSCALE
       FELL

● Millbeck

    Threlkeld ●

  ▲ LATRIGG

● Keswick

MILES

0 1 2 3 4

from the Orthwaite road

NATURAL FEATURES

Latrigg is to Keswick what Loughrigg is to Ambleside and Helm Crag to Grasmere : a small hill, an excellent viewpoint, a great favourite of local folk and visitors. Latrigg is pastoral and parkland in character, not rough fell, and the summit is the easiest of promenades, so that this is not a climb calling for old clothes and heavy boots : 'Sunday best' is quite appropriate dress. The woods, once a haven for courting couples and other wildlife, are privately owned, being part of the Mirehouse Estate, and in recent years they have been increasingly managed for the benefit of walkers. There are three information panels, and a circular walk has been created. It heads east from Spoony Green for two miles and returns at a lower level. A leaflet is available at the Tourist Information Centre in Keswick.

Latrigg has been well described as 'the cub of Skiddaw'. It crouches at the foot of the broad southern slopes of the parent, too small to be significant in the geography of the mass, although a long east ridge is reponsible for the formation of the short side-valley of Lonscale.   The River Greta flows along the southern base, occupying a wooded gorge of outstanding scenic beauty, appreciated best from the disused railway from Keswick to Threlkeld.

1 : The summit
2 : East ridge
3 : Brundholme Woods
4 : Slope of
        Skiddaw Little Man
5 : Slope of
        Lonscale Fell
6 : Glenderaterra Beck
7 : Lonscale Valley (below)
8 : River Greta
9 : Gale Gill

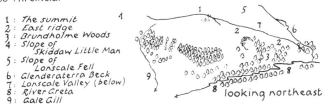

looking northeast

Latrigg's top is a smooth grassy pasture innocent of rock except for a few yards of outcrop at the summit where the native stone breaks through the turf.   This is seen to be slate. The wall across the top to the east is built of slate.

Not long ago, in fact since the turn of the 20th century, Latrigg's top was described as having a scattering of boulders of volcanic rock deposited there by a retreating glacier.   These boulders were identified as having their origin in the crags of Clough Head and it is therefore simple to reconstruct (but difficult to imagine) the scene here at the end of the Ice Age : the glacier tore from its moorings in the narrows of St. John's Vale, and, taking the route of the present St. John's Beck and River Greta and being joined by tributaries of ice from the Glenderamackin, the Glenderaterra and the Naddle Valleys, slowly withdrew from the hills, scouring the side of Lonscale Fell and Skiddaw and depositing the rubble collected on its journey as it disintegrated. The presence of Clough Head rocks on the top of Latrigg indicates that the surface of the glacier must have been higher than the present elevation of the fell.

These boulders have now gone, possibly removed with the trees to make a smooth sheepwalk. Just a few 'erratics' can still be found by diligent search, but the evidence of the movement of the glacier is more abundant lower down the fellside and about the bed of the Greta, where, to a trained eye, there are several manifestations of glacial action, much of it unearthed during the construction of the railway.

MAP

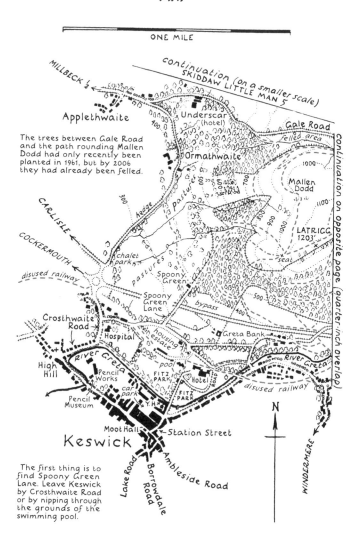

ONE MILE

MILLBECK ½

Applethwaite

continuation (on a smaller scale)
SKIDDAW LITTLE MAN 5

Underscar
(hotel)

Gale Road

felled area

The trees between Gale Road
and the path rounding Mallen
Dodd had only recently been
planted in 1961, but by 2006
they had already been felled.

Ormathwaite

1000

Mallen
Dodd

CARLISLE

COCKERMOUTH

hedge

pasture

300

1100

LATRIGG
1203'

800
900
1000

seat

disused railway

chalet
park

pastures

Spoony
Green

Spoony
Green
Lane

bypass

500

400

Crosthwaite
Road

Hospital

housing
estate

Greta Bank

High
Hill

River Greta

Pencil
Works

pool

FITZ
PARK

Hotel

River Greta

disused railway

Pencil
Museum

car
park

Y.H.

FITZ
PARK

N

Moot Hall

Station Street

Keswick

Lake Road

Borrowdale
Road

Ambleside Road

WINDERMERE

The first thing is to
find Spoony Green
Lane. Leave Keswick
by Crosthwaite Road
or by nipping through
the grounds of the
swimming pool.

MAP

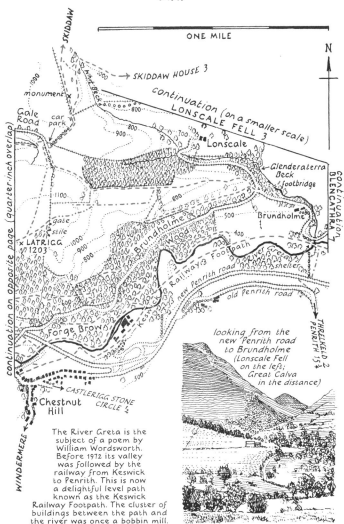

ONE MILE

N

looking from the
new Penrith road
to Brundholme
(Lonscale Fell
on the left;
Great Calva
in the distance)

The River Greta is the
subject of a poem by
William Wordsworth.
Before 1972 its valley
was followed by the
railway from Keswick
to Penrith. This is now
a delightful level path
known as the Keswick
Railway Footpath. The cluster of
buildings between the path and
the river was once a bobbin mill.

ASCENT FROM KESWICK
950 feet of ascent: 2½ miles

The original path, rounding Mallen Dodd, is the easiest route to the top, but there are a number of short-cuts. The start of Route A is easily missed. It leaves the main path by a gate post at the end of a short stretch of fence. For Route B turn sharp right onto a forest road and then turn left after passing through a gate. This route is best avoided because of a difficult stretch just below the fence. Route C leaves the main path shortly after it crosses a stream. All these paths are provided with stiles where they cross the forest fence. At the time of writing this is a good place to see red squirrels, but in a few years they will probably all be gone.

Happily, the superb view from the summit is available also to non-climbers, and the old and infirm, with the assistance of a car, can enjoy it by a simple stroll from the road end.

Road end
Cars may be taken to this point (via Underscar) and parked here

LATRIGG

SKIDDAW

Gate Road UNDERSCAR

gate post   Mallen Dodd

grass

1100...×seat

ridge

1000

900

C   B

800

A

700

looking east

Ewe How (viewpoint)

500

gate post

bypass

Just above Spoony Green is an interesting notice board with paintings of wildlife and information about Latrigg Woods.

Spoony Green

500

Spoony Green Lane

CARLISLE

housing estate

There is a bewildering choice of paths, that by Mallen Dodd being best. The descent by the east ridge and return to Keswick by Brundholme Woods completes a very beautiful short walk.

Pheasant Inn

Crosthwaite Road

Hospital

River Greta

Keswick

ASCENT FROM THRELKELD
900 feet of ascent : 3 miles

This simple climb by the east ridge can be made with equal facility from Keswick. Take the road behind the swimming pool signposted "Windebrowe & Brundholme" — this degenerates into a lane but improves in scenery as it enters and passes through the woods: a delightful walk with interesting glimpses of the River Greta below.

From Threlkeld, the bridge over Glenderaterra Beck is reached along the road signposted "Wescoe & Derwent Folds", turning down a lane to the left at Wescoe. This bridge can also be reached from Keswick by the Keswick Railway Footpath, turning left just before the shelter.

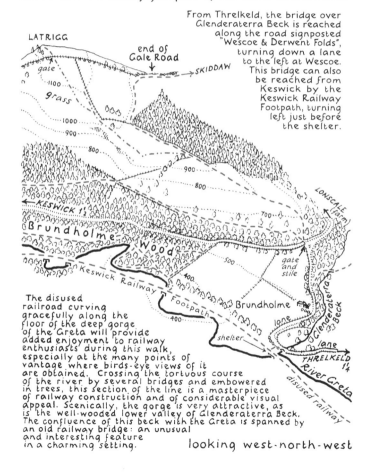

The disused railroad curving gracefully along the floor of the deep gorge of the Greta will provide added enjoyment to railway enthusiasts during this walk, especially at the many points of vantage where birds-eye views of it are obtained. Crossing the tortuous course of the river by several bridges and embowered in trees, this section of the line is a masterpiece of railway construction and of considerable visual appeal. Scenically, the gorge is very attractive, as is the well-wooded lower valley of Glenderaterra Beck. The confluence of this beck with the Greta is spanned by an old railway bridge: an unusual and interesting feature in a charming setting.

looking west-north-west

Underskiddaw, looking to Bassenthwaite Lake

.... Two views from Latrigg ....

Blease Fell, Blencathra, from the east ridge

THE SUMMIT

The top of Latrigg is a green sward, crossed by an excellent gravel path that runs along the top of a causeway. 150 yards west of the summit the path passes almost over the top of a little rocky knoll where there are good views of Keswick and Derwent Water. 100 yards farther west is a seat in a commanding position bearing the inscription 'a 90th birthday tribute to Ronald Lupton of Keswick 23/7/91'. The area was once covered in trees, but now only a pine and two larches remain; even the stumps have gone.

The top of Latrigg is a grand place, especially for fellwalkers on the retired list: here they can recline for hours, recalling joyful days when they had energy enough to climb to the tops of all the mountains in view. Strange how all the best days of memory are to do with summit-cairns...... Will there be mountains like these in heaven...... or is *this* heaven, before death, and will there never again be hills to climb? Is Latrigg the last of all? But no, it needn't be — there's still Orrest Head, even easier...... Funny, *that's* where we came in ......

The Grasmoor group, from Gale Road

THE VIEW

There is complete contrast between the northern and southern halves of the view. The northern, consisting of featureless slopes sweeping up to a high skyline, will hardly get a second glance unless the ling is in bloom, but to the south is a panorama of crowded detail, all of it of great beauty: indeed, this scene is one of the gems of the district. The roofs of Keswick are below, Derwent Water is set out just beyond, in its lovely entirety, and in the distance Borrowdale and the Newlands Valley are seen winding deeply amongst the sombre mountains. The far horizon is a jumbled upheaval of peaks, with many dear old friends standing up proudly: Helvellyn, Bowfell, the Scafells, Great Gable, Pillar, the Buttermere fells, and, much nearer, the striking outline of the Grasmoor group. There is enough of interest in this charming picture to engage the attention for many hours, and Latrigg is a place to visit time and time again, for the scene is never quite the same but always fresh and exciting. The view is so much the best reason for climbing Latrigg that it is almost a pity to make the ascent on a day of poor visibility.

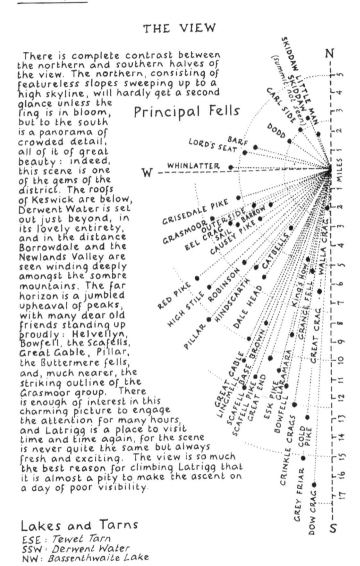

Principal Fells

Lakes and Tarns

ESE: *Tewet Tarn*
SSW: *Derwent Water*
NW: *Bassenthwaite Lake*

THE VIEW

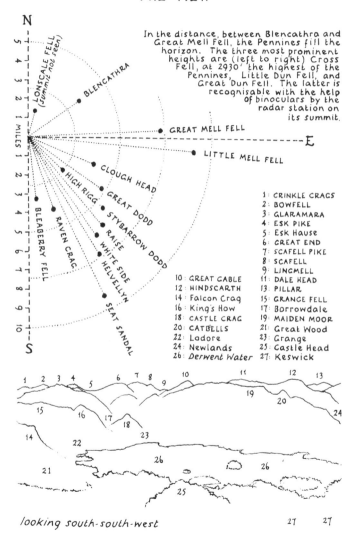

In the distance, between Blencathra and Great Mell Fell, the Pennines fill the horizon. The three most prominent heights are (left to right) Cross Fell, at 2930' the highest of the Pennines, Little Dun Fell, and Great Dun Fell. The latter is recognisable with the help of binoculars by the radar station on its summit.

LONSCALE FELL (summit not seen)

BLENCATHRA

GREAT MELL FELL

LITTLE MELL FELL

CLOUGH HEAD

HIGH RIGG

GREAT DODD

STYBARROW DODD

RAISE

WHITE SIDE

HELVELLYN

RAVEN CRAG

BLEABERRY FELL

SEAT SANDAL

1: CRINKLE CRAGS
2: BOWFELL
3: GLARAMARA
4: ESK PIKE
5: ESK HAUSE
6: GREAT END
7: SCAFELL PIKE
8: SCAFELL
9: LINGMELL
10: GREAT GABLE
11: DALE HEAD
12: HINDSCARTH
13: PILLAR
14: Falcon Crag
15: GRANGE FELL
16: King's How
17: Borrowdale
18: CASTLE CRAG
19: MAIDEN MOOR
20: CATBELLS
21: Great Wood
22: Ladore
23: Grange
24: Newlands
25: Castle Head
26: *Derwent Water*
27: Keswick

looking south-south-west

135

11 Causey Pike
from Stair

One of the biggest challenges for parents leading walks is to convince their children that the summit is not too far off and that they might, with a bit of effort and coaxing, reach their target before long. But too often in the Lake District their arguments are let down by the highest point being hidden from view by a succession of 'false' summits – leaving children increasingly sceptical that the top even exists, or that they are ever going to get their lunch and a rest.

There are no such problems with Causey Pike. The rocky top of this excellent fell is in view for just about all of the ascent from the road, and children will have no cause for complaining that it is further than they were told. The fell's distinctive top and neat, pyramid shape also make it an instantly recognisable fell, strikingly different from many in the Lakes that can be difficult to distinguish from one another. The differences extend to the wider summit area, which is a short, bumpy crest, and there are wonderful views over dozens of fells and a couple of valleys.

The steep sides and rocky top suggest a challenging climb, but Causey Pike is within the reach of most walkers in a morning or afternoon, and it makes a fine introduction to more substantial – though no more attractive – fells elsewhere in Newlands. This walk combines Wainwright's two suggested routes from Stair at the start of the picturesque Newlands valley, taking the direct route up and returning via a lovely ridge walk to Rowling End. The final stretch up, from where the two paths meet at Sleet Hause, involves some light rock climbing that most children will be able to negotiate with ease. The route through the rocks is easier than it was in Wainwright's day, with the way up now very well trodden and clear to follow, though coming down sections like these always requires more care than going up, and small children or adults with babies in carriers might prefer to wait at the foot of this short last scramble. Though anyone who baulks at this or any other point might like to know that Causey Pike hosts a race for fellrunners every spring – and that the winners usually make it all the way up and down in about half an hour.

From *Book Six: The North Western Fells*

Distance 3 miles (4.8km)

Ascent 1,750 feet (535m)

Start and finish point The car park by Newlands Village Hall in Stair (NY 237 212)

Ordnance Survey maps Explorer OL4; Landranger 89 or 90

Getting there

Stair is a small village south of Braithwaite on the road through the Newlands valley. From Keswick, take the Portinscale turn off the A66 and follow the signs for Swinside then Stair. If the Village Hall car park is full, park with care on the verges alongside the building, or follow the early directions of the walk and look for roadside spaces. (Parking by the cattle-grid will shorten the walk by about ½ mile, though spaces there are limited and the way up the road on foot is very pleasant.) In return for parking at the Village Hall, donations are invited towards its upkeep; they can be posted through the letterbox in the door.

Buses do not pass through Stair, but the 77 service calls close by. It runs four times a day from early April to early November inclusive in either direction on a loop from Keswick that takes in Seatoller, Buttermere and Whinlatter; take the clockwise direction if embarking from Keswick. Ask for the Swinside or Hawse End drop-offs; both are just under 1 mile of walking from Stair. Hawse End is also served by the ferry service across

Derwent Water, and the ten-minute ride across the lake from Keswick makes a very pleasant start to the walk. Summer services run about every hour in each direction around Derwent Water, though they are much reduced in the winter; take the anti-clockwise boat and check times in advance to plan your day (017687 72263, www.keswick-launch.co.uk).

Facilities, food and drink

The nearest food and drink to Stair can be found about ½ mile away at the only pub in the Newlands valley, the Swinside Inn, a nice Lakeland inn with rooms and an outdoor area (017687 78253, www.theswinsideinn.com). Most of the other buildings in Newlands are farms or holiday cottages, and the nearest places for stocking up with a picnic or refreshments before or after the walk are Keswick, which has a host of pubs, cafés and shops to choose from; and Portinscale, which has a village shop (017687 75307) and a pub (The Farmers Arms; 017687 72322).

For family activities beyond the walk, head for Keswick. Anyone wanting to combine Lake District walking with some water-based sports will find this a good place to start. There are several operators providing hire and instruction for boating, canoeing, windsurfing and other activities on Derwent Water, including a couple at Portinscale: the Derwent Water Marina (017687 72912, www.derwentwatermarina.co.uk) and Nichol End Marine (017687 73082, www.nicholendmarine.co.uk). Phone in advance to discuss activities or turn up on the day. The area along this shore and through the Newlands valley is also famous as the inspiration for many characters and settings of Beatrix Potter's Tales, as she used to holiday close by.

Directions

1 Turn right out of the Village Hall car park to drop down to the T-junction in front of playing fields. Turn left and follow the road over a bridge and uphill, until it reaches a cattle-grid ¼

mile on. About 50m further from this, look for a path through the bracken on your right, and follow it to immediately meet another road. Cross this and pick up the path opposite, cutting half left through more bracken. Within another 50m the path meets two junctions, the second with a grassy path; go straight over both of them to continue ascending. Just over 100m further, at another fork, take the right-hand path to traverse the hillside and then join a clearer path that starts to rise up again.

2 The way is now very clear, making directly towards the unmistakable knobbly top of Causey Pike in front of you and with a stream, Stonycroft Gill, down to the right. About ½ mile on from the last fork, and after a series of zig-zags among heather, the path reaches a cairn by a junction of paths called Sleet Hause (NY 222 207). Bear right for the final ¼ mile pull up to the summit, which is guarded by a rocktower that requires some scrambling. Most children will enjoy picking their way up, but for an easier way to the top, bear left just in front of the rocks and tackle it from the other side, or leave it altogether. The scramble leads to a lovely grassy summit area (NY 219 209). See Wainwright's notes for more about the distinctive summit ridge and the confusion about its highest point.

3 Pick your way back down the rocks with great care, and retrace your steps back to the cairn at Sleet Hause. Here, instead of returning along the direct route, bear right to pick up the fine ridge path through heather, with terrific views all around. The path is very clear and remains largely level for a little under ½ mile until it reaches the end of the ridge at a grassy patch called Rowling End (NY 229 207), before dropping more steeply downhill. The obvious path eventually reaches the junction of ways met earlier. Retrace your steps from here, or pick another way through the criss-crossing paths laid out beneath you back to the road, which is followed back down to Stair and the car park.

Causey Pike

2090'

Braithwaite
●

▲ GRISEDALE PIKE

● Stair

EEL
▲ CRAG

▲ CAUSEY PIKE

MILES

0 1 2 3

from Swinside

NATURAL FEATURES

Most fells conform to a general pattern, but some have an unorthodoxy of shape, a peculiarity of outline, that identifies them on sight from wherever they may be seen. These not only help to fix a bearing in moments of doubt but serve also as pointers to neighbouring fells not favoured with distinctive features.

A landmark of this kind is Causey Pike, dominant in the Newlands and Derwent Water scene. The knob of the summit would itself be enough for identification in most views; repeated four times in lesser undulations as it is, like the legendary sea-serpent, the top is quite unmistakable. Even when the lesser ups and downs are concealed from sight, as when the fell is seen end on, the pyramid of the main summit is no less impressive because then it gains in slimness and elegance.

Causey Pike rises very sharply from Newlands but the steepness abates on Rowling End at 1400', whence a half-mile ridge continues easily to Sleet Hause, just below the final tower, where the steepness recurs on a narrowing crest. Rock is in evidence here, and must be handled to attain the summit. Thereafter the top of the fell is a succession of gentle undulations leading on to Scar Crags and the fine ridge that climbs up to Eel Crag and descends beyond to Crummock Water.

Bracken clothes the lower slopes and heather the higher. The confining streams are Stonycroft Beck and Rigg Beck, both feeders of Newlands Beck.

from Whiteless Breast

looking up the valley of
Sail Beck, with Eel Crag
and Sail on the left and
Ard Crags on the right

from Little Town

Causey Pike belongs wholly and exclusively to Newlands but peeps over the watershed of the Cocker, southwest, at several points.

MAP

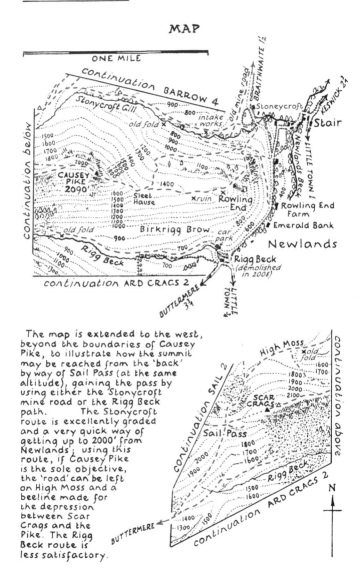

The map is extended to the west, beyond the boundaries of Causey Pike, to illustrate how the summit may be reached from the 'back' by way of Sail Pass (at the same altitude), gaining the pass by using either the Stonycroft mine road or the Rigg Beck path. The Stonycroft route is excellently graded and a very quick way of getting up to 2000' from Newlands; using this route, if Causey Pike is the sole objective, the 'road' can be left on High Moss and a beeline made for the depression between Scar Crags and the Pike. The Rigg Beck route is less satisfactory.

ASCENT FROM STAIR
1750 feet of ascent : 1½ miles

From Sleet Hause to the summit the way lies up the sharp east-south-east ridge: a delightful climb. The final rocktower requires the use of hands: it is easy, but no place for fooling about.

The direct route gains the ridge at Sleet Hause and a splendid view suddenly unfolds to the south.

CAUSEY PIKE

1900
1800 heather
1700
1600
1500

Sleet Hause

indistinct junction

Rowling End

heather
1400
1300
1200
1100
1000

heather

bracken

grass path
900
800 bracken
700

old fold

Ellas Crag

bracken
wide grass path
BUTTERMERE 4½

direct route

600

500

gorge
Stonycroft Gill → SAIL PASS

mine road
ROAD

400

Stair Mill

Stonycroft

The mine road offers a long but very easy alternative route, reaching Causey Pike from the 'back' via Scar Crags

car park
BRAITHWAITE 1¼

Stair

Newlands Beck

car park

→ KESWICK 3

looking south-west

For sustained interest and beauty of views, the Rowling End route is to be preferred; this is the original path but now it is mostly used in descending by walkers who have missed the bifurcation of the direct route on Sleet Hause.

Deservedly this is a popular climb, with a heavy summer traffic, the route being quite charming, the views superlative, the finish a bit of real mountaineering, and the summit a place of distinctive character.

ASCENT FROM BRAITHWAITE
2150 feet of ascent : 4½ miles (via Sail Pass)

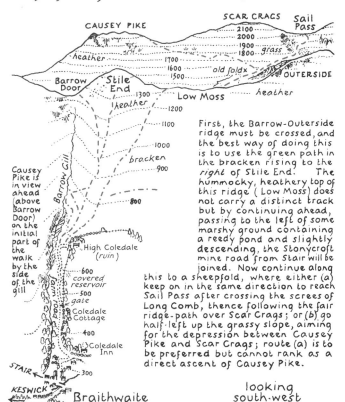

First, the Barrow-Outside ridge must be crossed, and the best way of doing this is to use the green path in the bracken rising to the *right* of Stile End. The hummocky, heathery top of this ridge (Low Moss) does not carry a distinct track but by continuing ahead, passing to the left of some marshy ground containing a reedy pond and slightly descending, the Stonycroft mine road from Stair will be joined. Now continue along this to a sheepfold, where either (a) keep on in the same direction to reach Sail Pass after crossing the screes of Long Comb, thence following the fair ridge-path over Scar Crags; or (b) go half-left up the grassy slope, aiming for the depression between Causey Pike and Scar Crags; route (a) is to be preferred but cannot rank as a direct ascent of Causey Pike.

looking
south-west

Causey Pike is clearly in view from Braithwaite, and its quaint and challenging outline makes it an obvious objective for a day's walk. The route, however, is somewhat 'artificial', as an intervening ridge must first be crossed, and a better plan is to ascend direct from Stair, using the above route for the return journey.

THE SUMMIT

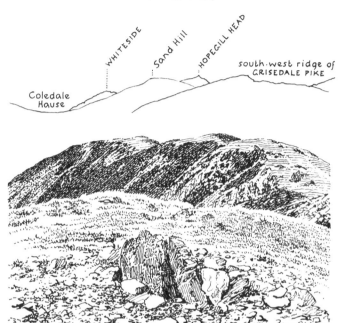

WHITESIDE

Sand Hill

HOPEGILL HEAD

south-west ridge of GRISEDALE PIKE

Coledale Hause

This delightful 'top' is quite unlike any other, its narrow crest undulating over five distinct bumps (meticulous visitors will count seven), the most prominent being the one terminating so abruptly the eastern end of the crest: this is the rocky knob that identifies Causey Pike unmistakably in distant views of the fell. The eastern knob appears to have a slight advantage in altitude, a matter of a few feet or even inches only, over the third bump — the second bump is clearly lower. The third, fourth and fifth bumps have piles of stones on their summits, that on the fourth bump being the largest.

DESCENTS : Leave the top by the path down the east-south-east ridge from the eastern knob; this is rocky at first, needing care in bad conditions, and is not pleasant to descend. At the foot of the steep section, on Sleet Hause, the direct route to Stair goes off to the left at once and the original path over Rowling End continues ahead, the bifurcation at this point being indistinct. It is advisable to use the direct route: the way off Rowling End is on a plain but abominably rough path with no alternative possible.

THE VIEW

In all directions the scenery is of the highest order.
  Predominantly the view is of mountains, but the severity and starkness of their outlines is softened by the verdant loveliness of the Vales of Keswick and Newlands. Nothing is better than the challenging ridge continuing to Eel Crag. The head of Newlands, displaying the great humps of Dale Head, Hindscarth and Robinson — a magnificent grouping — is exceptionally well seen. The several Pikes of Scafell appear from this viewpoint as separate mountains.

Principal Fells

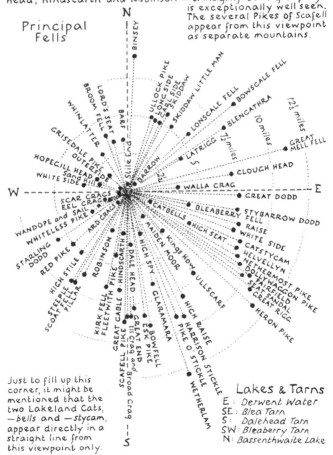

Just to fill up this corner, it might be mentioned that the two Lakeland Cats, —bells and —stycam, appear directly in a straight line from this viewpoint only.

Lakes & Tarns
E: Derwent Water
SE: Blea Tarn
S: Dalehead Tarn
SW: Bleaberry Tarn
N: Bassenthwaite Lake

146

RIDGE ROUTE

To SCAR CRAGS, 2205': ¾ mile: WNW, then W.
Depression at 1915': 320 feet of ascent

Traverse all the bumps and descend a wide stony path to the depression beyond. The ragged edge of Scar Crags now rears imposingly ahead, but the rising track alongside has no difficulties and the flat top is reached after a simple climb, during which striking downward views are available on the left.

HALF A MILE

looking back to Causey Pike from the depression

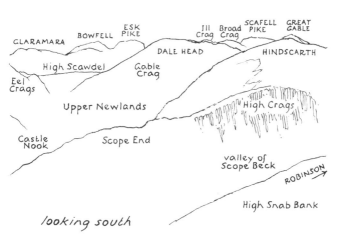

looking south

The valley of Rigg Beck, from Causey Pike

The ridge west from Causey Pike

Key to drawings

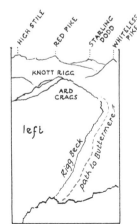

HIGH STILE • RED PIKE • STARLING DODD • WHITELESS PIKE

KNOTT RIGG

ARD CRAGS

left

Rigg Beck

path to Buttermere

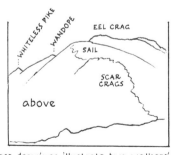

WHITELESS PIKE • WANDOPE • EEL CRAG

SAIL

SCAR CRAGS

above

These drawings illustrate two walkers'
ways from Newlands to Buttermere.
That via Rigg Beck is suitable for a wet
day, but the route *par excellence* in clear
weather is the ridge from Causey Pike to
Whiteless Pike — a magnificent walk.

12 Mellbreak

from Loweswater

There are no such things as undiscovered parts of the Lake District these days, but Loweswater remains one of its least explored corners. Some of the best walking in the Lakes is to be had around here, both on the flat and up in the fells that radiate out from the village, and yet it remains relatively free from the development and influx of visitors that have so changed other villages and towns.

Along with Low Fell, covered in Chapter 15 of this book, Mellbreak is a classic Loweswater walk. Viewed from ground level it seems a dramatic and daunting fell, looming steeply out of the village and Crummock Water in a classic alpine shape that suggests it will be impossible to climb. But while care is needed and it might be out of the reach of less confident walkers, it is an easier ascent than it appears, and a great choice for older children who want a challenge. The only difficulties are close to the start of the ascent over scree slopes, which are easier than in Wainwright's day thanks to the feet of decades of walkers, but which still require close attention and a bit of wayfinding to determine the best way forward. Beyond that, the climb to the top requires a little puff but is perfectly manageable and, with steep views down over the lake, delightful.

This walk up Mellbreak follows Wainwright's suggested direct ascent, and is extended from the obvious up-and-down by some stretches on the flat at the start and finish, first in the fields and woods near Loweswater and later along the Mosedale valley beside the river. All walks are better in good weather, of course, but this one is particularly worth saving for warm summer days, when the sun glints on the water and heather smothers the upper slopes.

From *Book Seven: The Western Fells*

Distance 3½ miles (5.6km)

Ascent 1,300 feet (400m)

Start and finish point The Kirkstile Inn in Loweswater (NY 141 209)

Ordnance Survey maps Explorer OL4; Landranger 89

Getting there

One of the reasons for Loweswater's tranquility is its relatively isolated situation – at least when arriving from the south, from which most people drive via Buttermere. Access from the north is easier, as the village can be reached from the A5086 that runs south from Cockermouth and the A66. Drivers from Keswick often prefer this route to crossing either the Whinlatter or Honister Passes.

Parking in Loweswater can be difficult, especially in the summer, when the limited spaces fill up quickly. The Kirkstile Inn is happy for people to use its good-sized car park if they eat or drink there before or after their walk, which most will want to do. Cars can also be left carefully on verges nearby. If you arrive early enough you may be able secure one of the few roadside spaces by Church Bridge close to the start of the walk, and there is more public parking by Maggie's Bridge, accessed via a narrow lane on the road linking Loweswater village and lake (NY 135 211) – though again there are only a few spaces.

Loweswater is not served by any buses. The closest it is possible to get is just over 1 mile away on the B5289 between Lorton and Buttermere, which is covered by the 77 service that runs on a loop from Keswick from early April to early November, four times each day in each direction. Ask for the Lanthwaite stop and follow the footpaths over to Loweswater.

Facilities, food and drink

The Kirkstile Inn is the only place to find food and drink in Loweswater – so it is fortunate that it is one of Cumbria's best pubs (01900 85219, www.kirkstile.com). It is a traditional

Lakeland inn with a fine outdoor terrace for the summer and roaring log fires in the winter, plus baby-changing facilities and a family-friendly dining room with books and games. With plenty of rooms and self-catering accommodation, it makes a great place to stay. Note the pub's stuffed fox, a trophy from a long-running local fox hunt.

Beyond this, the nearest food and drink is at the Barn Tearooms at New House Farm near Brackenthwaite (07841 159818, www.newhouse-farm.com). The closest pubs are in Buttermere and, to the north, the Wheatsheaf Inn in Low Lorton (01900 85199, www.wheatsheafinnlorton.co.uk). Loweswater's church – which seems rather large for such a small community, because it was expanded in the late 19th century ahead of an anticipated mining-related population boom that never came – is also worth a visit.

Directions

1 Walk downhill on the road between the church and the Kirkstile Inn to reach a road junction by the river and a signpost offering two unpromising alternatives: 'No road to the lake' and 'No through road'. Follow the first of these to pick up a quiet, narrow road down for about ¼ mile to a junction, and turn right. It crosses Park Bridge and splits into two rougher tracks; take the right-hand option, signposted for Ennerdale Water. After about 100m the path curves to the right of a building and then leads between two dry stone walls up to a wooden gate. Go through and take the grassy path uphill through the trees, soon bending to the right to hug the line of a wall. The wall, then a fence, is now within touching distance, with trees enclosed on the other side. Where the fence is interrupted by a gap and a lane leading back to Loweswater (NY 139 201), leave it to the left to climb up the grassy slopes.

2 The path strikes through bracken at first, then reaches a scree slope. Follow the zig-zagging path that has been fashioned roughly out of the middle of it, and keep a close eye on children as you do so. The stones eventually taper out and give way to a path through heather, continuing to rise steeply. (Do not branch off into the heather too early, but instead carry on upwards until the scree diminishes.) The path passes a couple of flatter points with fine views (and steep drops around; again take care with children) before picking up a more defined stone gully through the heather and rising up to a broader promontory at a height of just above 1,300 feet (NY 143 199). Another short but sharp pull up leads to the summit area, and a flatter stroll through it arrives at the northern – and better – of the two tops described by Wainwright in his notes (NY 143 195).

3 Continue directly ahead from the first cairn reached, ignoring side-paths to the left and a second, competing cairn on the right. The path, marshy in places, drops down to a depression, with the second, southern summit of Mellbreak directly ahead. (This is the higher of the two tops by a few feet, so anyone keen to bag the 'proper' peak can do so here, though it is hardly worth the effort.) After just over 500m, at the lowest point of the depression (NY 145 190), look for a faint junction of paths and take the fork branching right. It runs roughly in parallel with the summit path at first, but just under 200m on, ahead of a gully in the fellside, follow the split in the path to curve round to the right. This drops down more steeply all the way to the valley floor (NY 142 186).

4 Turn right along the path along the valley, and just under 200m further on bear right on to the more distinct track, now with a fence to your left and Mosedale Beck beyond. After ¾ mile it reaches a junction of paths; bear left on the main track, now with pine trees on your right. Just under ¼ mile further, cross through a wooden gate (NY 139 202) and follow the winding lane between dry stone walls. Another ½ mile of walking reaches Loweswater, the track having become a road, crossed Park Beck over Church Bridge, and emerged into the village at the signpost by the Kirkstile Inn.

Mellbreak

1676'

from Kirkhead

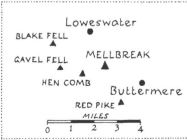

Loweswater ●

BLAKE FELL ▲

GAVEL FELL ▲   MELLBREAK ▲

HEN COMB ▲

RED PIKE ▲   Buttermere ●

MILES

0   1   2   3   4

In West Cumbria, where Mellbreak is a household word (largely through long association with the Melbreak Foxhounds (spelt with one 'l')) the fell is highly esteemed, and there have always been people ready to assert that it is the finest of all. This is carrying local patriotism too far, but nevertheless it is a grand hill in a beautiful situation with a character all its own and an arresting outline not repeated in the district.

There is only one Mellbreak.

NATURAL FEATURES

There is, of course, a natural affinity between mountains and lakes; they have developed side by side in the making of the earth. Often there is a special association between a particular mountain and a particular lake, so that, in calling the one to mind the other comes inevitably to mind also: they belong together. The best example of this is provided by Wast Water and the Screes, and perhaps next best is the combination of Mellbreak and Crummock Water, essential partners in a successful scenery enterprise, depending on each other for effectiveness. Crummock Water's eastern shore, below Grasmoor, is gay with life and colour — trees, pastures, farms, cattle, traffic, tents and people — but it is the view across the lake, where the water laps the sterile base of Mellbreak far beneath the mountain's dark escarpment, where loneliness, solitude and silence prevail, that makes the scene unforgettable.

Mellbreak, seen thus, is a grim sight, the austere effect often heightened by shadow, and a much closer examination is needed to reveal the intimate detail of crag and gully and scree, the steep declivities cushioned in heather, the hidden corners and recesses, the soaring ravens of Raven Crag. From Kirkstile, at the northern foot, the gable of the fell assumes the arresting outline of a towering pyramid, suggesting a narrow crest, but the top widens into a considerable plateau having two summits of almost equal height separated by a broad saddle. Symmetry and simplicity are the architectural *motifs*, and the steep flank above Crummock Water has its counterpart to the west descending to the dreariest and wettest of Lakeland's many Mosedales. Thus the severance from other fells is complete. Mellbreak is isolated, independent of other high ground, aloof.

Its one allegiance is to Crummock Water.

from Scalehill Bridge

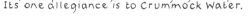

MAP

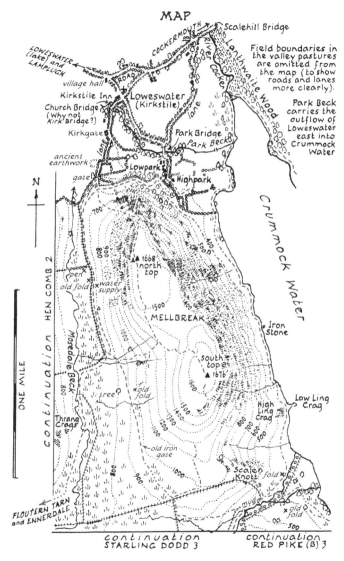

Field boundaries in the valley pastures are omitted from the map (to show roads and lanes more clearly).

Park Beck carries the outflow of Loweswater east into Crummock Water

SCALEHILL BRIDGE

COCKERMOUTH

River Cocker

Lanthwaite Wood

LOWESWATER (lake) and LAMPLUGH

village hall

ROAD

Kirkstile Inn

Loweswater (Kirkstile)

Church Bridge (Why not Kirk Bridge?)

lane

Kirkgate

Park Bridge Park Beck

lane

ancient earthwork

Lowpark

gate

Highpark

N

Crummock Water

700

900

800

▲ 1668 north top

400

pen

old fold × water supply

1500

MELLBREAK

Iron Stone

CONTINUATION HEN COMB 2

Mosedale Beck

1000

south top

▲ 1676

800

ONE MILE

tree

× old fold

1600

1500

1400

Low Ling Crag

High Ling Crag

Thrang Crags

1300

1200

800

700

500

old iron gate

1100

1000

900

800

Scalen Knott

fold ×

FLOUTERN TARN and ENNERDALE

800

700

500

×old fold

mvg

500

continuation STARLING DODD 3

continuation RED PIKE (B) 3

".... *a lovely peep around a corner....*"
(direct ascent from Loweswater)

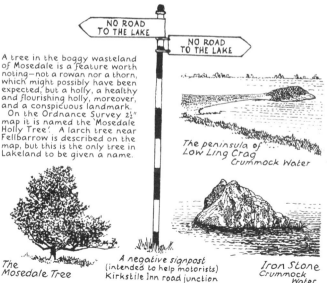

A tree in the boggy wasteland of Mosedale is a feature worth noting—not a rowan nor a thorn, which might possibly have been expected, but a holly, a healthy and flourishing holly, moreover, and a conspicuous landmark.
  On the Ordnance Survey 2½" map it is named the 'Mosedale Holly Tree'. A larch tree near Fellbarrow is described on the map, but this is the only tree in Lakeland to be given a name.

NO ROAD TO THE LAKE

NO ROAD TO THE LAKE

The peninsula of
Low Ling Crag
Crummock Water

The
Mosedale Tree

A negative signpost
(intended to help motorists)
Kirkstile Inn road junction

Iron Stone
Crummock
Water

157

ASCENT (to the north top) FROM LOWESWATER
1300 feet of ascent : 1¼ miles

looking south

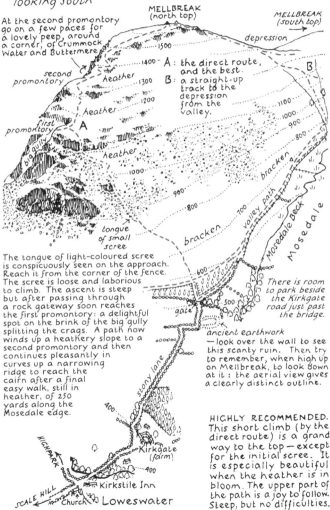

MELLBREAK
(north top)

MELLBREAK
(south top)

At the second promontory
go on a few paces for
a lovely peep, around
a corner, of Crummock
Water and Buttermere

depression

second
promontory

Heather

1500

1400

1300

A : the direct route,
and the best.

B : a straight-up
track to the
depression
from the
valley.

B

1200

first
promontory

A

Heather

1100

1000

900

800

Heather

big gully

1000

900

bracken

800

700

valley path

tongue
of small
scree

bracken

600

Mosedale Beck

Mosedale

The tongue of light-coloured scree
is conspicuously seen on the approach.
Reach it from the corner of the fence.
The scree is loose and laborious
to climb. The ascent is steep
but after passing through
a rock gateway soon reaches
the first promontory: a delightful
spot on the brink of the big gully
splitting the crags. A path now
winds up a heathery slope to a
second promontory and then
continues pleasantly in
curves up a narrowing
ridge to reach the
cairn after a final
easy walk, still in
heather, of 250
yards along the
Mosedale edge.

500

gate

There is room
to park beside
the Kirkgate
road just past
the bridge.

ancient earthwork
— look over the wall to see
this scanty ruin. Then try
to remember, when high up
on Mellbreak, to look down
at it: the aerial view gives
a clearly distinct outline.

stony lane

400

HIGHPARK

SCALE HILL

400

Kirkgate
(farm)

400

Kirkstile Inn

Church   Loweswater

HIGHLY RECOMMENDED.
This short climb (by the
direct route) is a grand
way to the top — except
for the initial scree. It
is especially beautiful
when the heather is in
bloom. The upper part of
the path is a joy to follow.
Steep, but no difficulties.

ASCENT FROM CRUMMOCK WATER
1350 feet of ascent : ¾ mile (to the north top).
1450 feet of ascent : 1 mile
(to the south top)

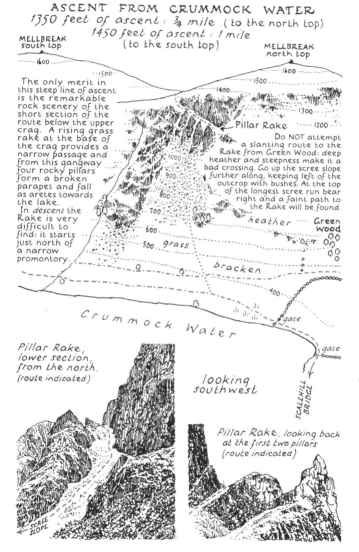

MELLBREAK south top

MELLBREAK north top

····· 1600 ·····

····· 1500 ·····

····· 1500 ·····

····· 1400 ····

····· 1600 ····

····· 1500 ····

····· 1200 ····

····· 1300 ····

The only merit in this steep line of ascent is the remarkable rock scenery of the short section of the route below the upper crag. A rising grass rake at the base of the crag provides a narrow passage and from this gangway four rocky pillars form a broken parapet and fall as aretes towards the lake.

In *descent* the Rake is very difficult to find: it starts just north of a narrow promontory.

← Pillar Rake

Do NOT attempt a slanting route to the Rake from Green Wood: deep heather and steepness make it a bad crossing. Go up the scree slope further along, keeping left of the outcrop with bushes. At the top of the longest scree run bear right and a faint path to the Rake will be found.

1000

900

800

700

600

500 grass

heather   Green Wood

bracken

400

Crummock Water

gate

gate

SCALEHILL BRIDGE

Pillar Rake, lower section, from the north. (route indicated)

looking southwest

SCREE SLOPE

Pillar Rake, looking back at the first two pillars (route indicated)

ASCENT (to the south top) FROM BUTTERMERE
1300 feet of ascent : 2½ miles

looking north-west

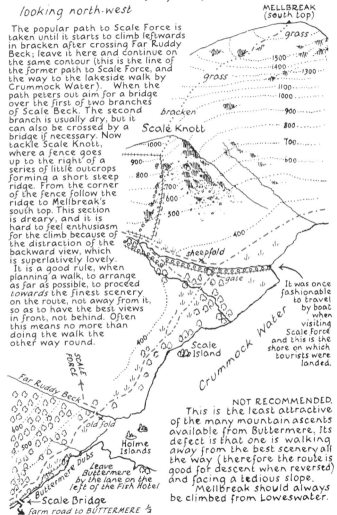

MELLBREAK
(south top)

The popular path to Scale Force is taken until it starts to climb leftwards in bracken after crossing Far Ruddy Beck; leave it here and continue on the same contour (this is the line of the former path to Scale Force, and the way to the lakeside walk by Crummock Water). When the path peters out aim for a bridge over the first of two branches of Scale Beck. The second branch is usually dry, but it can also be crossed by a bridge if necessary. Now tackle Scale Knott, where a fence goes up to the right of a series of little outcrops forming a short steep ridge. From the corner of the fence follow the ridge to Mellbreak's south top. This section is dreary, and it is hard to feel enthusiasm for the climb because of the distraction of the backward view, which is superlatively lovely.

It is a good rule, when planning a walk, to arrange as far as possible, to proceed *towards* the finest scenery on the route, not away from it, so as to have the best views in front, not behind. Often this means no more than doing the walk the other way round.

It was once fashionable to travel by boat when visiting Scale Force and this is the shore on which tourists were landed.

NOT RECOMMENDED. This is the least attractive of the many mountain ascents available from Buttermere. Its defect is that one is walking away from the best scenery all the way (therefore the route is good for descent when reversed) and facing a tedious slope.

Mellbreak should always be climbed from Loweswater.

Leave Buttermere by the lane on the left of the Fish Hotel

←Scale Bridge
farm road to BUTTERMERE ½

THE SUMMIT

HIGH STILE   RED PIKE   PILLAR

south top

Buttermere

1: FLEETWITH PIKE
2: GLARAMARA
3: GREY KNOTTS
4: BRANDRETH
5: GREEN GABLE
6: GREAT GABLE
7: HAYSTACKS

south-east
from the
north top

Mellbreak has two distinct summits, two-thirds of a mile apart and separated by a pronounced depression. The more attractive of the two is the heathery north top, measured by the Ordnance Survey as 1668 feet above sea level; the duller grassy south top is credited with 1676 feet. Nobody would have complained if the measurements had been reversed, by some rare error, for it is the lower north top, crowning a splendid tower of rock, that captures the fancy, not the other. The width and extent of the top of the fell between the two summits comes as a surprise — the narrow ridge promised by distant views of the fell is an illusion.

DESCENTS : It is usual to descend into Mosedale from the west edge of the depression. From the south top, for Buttermere, follow the ridge to the south until you come to a fence. Turn right to avoid the steep descent from Scale Knott, or turn left to avoid the mud along Scale Beck. For Loweswater, from the north top, the route from the depression into Mosedale is safest unless the direct route is already familiar and the weather clear: in mist, there is a very bad trap at the head of the big gully where a path along the promontory suggests a way down that can only lead to disaster; in fact the true path turns down left a few paces short of this point. On no account should a descent down the eastern flank to Crummock Water be attempted, except by Pillar Rake, and then only if the route is already known and the weather is clear. The start of the Rake, very difficult to find in descent, lies just north of a narrow promontory.

Dent   Floutern Cop

HEN COMB   GAVEL FELL

west
from the
south top

RIDGE ROUTES

Mellbreak is itself a ridge, like the keel of an overturned boat (collapsed in the middle). It has no links with other fells.

THE VIEW

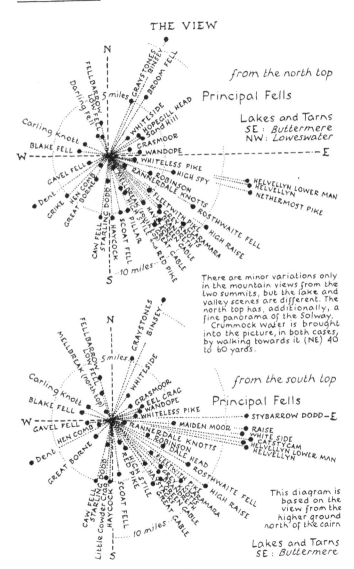

from the north top

Principal Fells

Lakes and Tarns
SE : *Buttermere*
NW : *Loweswater*

There are minor variations only in the mountain views from the two summits, but the lake and valley scenes are different. The north top has, additionally, a fine panorama of the Solway. Crummock Water is brought into the picture, in both cases, by walking towards it (NE) 40 to 60 yards.

from the south top

Principal Fells

This diagram is based on the view from the higher ground north of the cairn.

Lakes and Tarns
SE : *Buttermere*

Grasmoor
*from the
north top*

Rannerdale *from the south top*
(*Whiteless Pike, left background*)

13 Angletarn Pikes
from Patterdale

Angletarn Pikes has plenty to recommend it as a fell, with two striking summits that older children will enjoy scrambling up and splendid, differing views from each of them. The Pikes are a distinctive sight on the skyline, and scaling them makes for a fine sense of achievement despite their modest height. As Wainwright notes: 'This delightful walk should be in the itinerary of all who stay at Patterdale; the climb is pleasant and the views excellent.'

But it is the tarn that gives the fell its name that is the main attraction on this walk. In addition to its major lakes, Cumbria is dotted with several thousand tarns and pools, though the number fluctuates as landscapes change and the levels of rainfall or sunshine increase or decrease the tally. There are longer, wider and deeper tarns than Angle Tarn, though few are as dramatically located, nestling amid grassy slopes in a high basin not far from the top. 'The charms of Angle Tarn, at all seasons of the year, are manifold,' adds Wainwright. 'In scenic values it ranks amongst the best of Lakeland tarns.'

The tarn and its pair of small islands make for a fine sight from the Pikes, and it can be reached with a short, easy walk beyond the summit area. The water is home to diverse plant species and fish, while its shores make a fine spot for picnics and its edges are good for paddling. The tarn is popular among hardy wild swimmers and on warm days makes for a refreshing break after the walk up – though the usual safety precautions need to be taken before venturing in, especially with children, and even in the height of summer it is not a dip for the faint-hearted. Most walkers will be happy enough to enjoy the view.

This walk takes in both the Pikes and the Tarn from the direction of Patterdale, via the jumbled junction of walkers' paths at Boredale Hause – also a stopping point for Place Fell, featured in Chapter 20. The way up is straightforward until the final scramble at the Pikes, and some of the return stretch is on different, parallel paths for variety. The walk can be shortened by skipping the summits of either of the Pikes or the tarn, though all are worth the effort and should be within the reach of most children. For those with energy to go beyond Angle Tarn and turn the walk into a fuller day out, the path continues on towards High Street, the old Roman road linking forts at Penrith and Ambleside, and the fell of the same name.

From *Book Two: The Far Eastern Fells*

Distance 4 miles (6.4km)

Ascent 1,400 feet (425m)

Start and finish point The car park of the White Lion pub in Patterdale (NY 397 159)

Ordnance Survey maps Explorer OL5; Landranger 90

Getting there

Parking in Patterdale can be difficult, especially in the summer, as the village is the starting point for popular fells like Helvellyn. There are some roadside spaces and a small public car park, but they fill up very quickly, making the car park of the White Lion, close to the start of the walk, a better choice. Buy a ticket for the day from the pub itself, and return it later to get a full refund against any food or drink purchases. The car park is on the left at the head of the village as you arrive on the A592 from the Windermere direction; or the right at the far end of the village from Penrith and the north.

Alternatively, save on parking hassles altogether and take the bus. The 108 service serves Patterdale from Penrith via Pooley Bridge, while the 508 runs on to Windermere and

Bowness at weekends and in the summer holidays. From Keswick, the 208 bus delivers you to Patterdale. This is a walk that can be easily reached by train, since the 108 bus starts from Penrith train station, on the west coast main line.

Facilities, food and drink

The White Lion pub is recommended for food and drink, and not just because it means you can get your car park fee refunded. Walkers can buy packed lunches there before a day on the fells, and many gather there afterwards (017684 82214, www.thewhitelioninnpatterdale.co.uk). The Patterdale Village Store, very close to the car park, is another good place to put together a picnic for the walk (017684 82220).

Glenridding, a mile north on the A592, has pubs including The Travellers Rest (017684 82298) and The Glenridding Hotel (017684 82289, www.bw-glenriddinghotel.co.uk) and cafés including Fairlight (017684 82397, www.fairlightguesthouse. co.uk) and the aptly-named Fellbites (017684 82781). You can take a boat across the lake with Ullswater Steamers (017684 82229, www.ullswater-steamers.co.uk), and a Tourist Information Centre in the village's main car park will supply ideas for more things to do nearby (017684 82414). On a wet day, a good place to escape to is the Rheged Centre 12 miles north near Penrith, which has play areas, café, cinema, pottery painting workshop and lots more for children to do.

Directions

1 Return to the road from the car park, and turn right to walk away from the village in the direction of the Kirkstone Pass. By a Parish noticeboard, turn left down to a bridge over the river, Goldrill Bridge. Follow the narrow road up to a cluster of houses, where it forks. Bear left here, following the signs for Boredale Hause. Rise up to another junction, and leave the road through a wooden gate on to a track, again signposted for Boredale Hause. After a couple of zig-zags the path splits;

turn right. About 150m further on, at another junction, bear left and soon rise up to a green bench. The path now climbs steadily. Ignoring all side-paths to your left, continue ahead for just under ½ mile to a depression marked with a cairn (NY 407 156). This is part of Boredale Hause, a spaghetti junction of walkers' paths.

2 Immediately after the cairn the path forks into three. Take the right-hand option to climb up Angletarn Pikes. The path soon passes between two steep crags, then picks up a succession of cairns. Just over ½ mile from Boredale Hause it forks; take the left-hand path here to continue climbing. The path now skirts round the Pikes and eventually brings Angle Tarn into view beneath you. If you want to reach the top of either or both of the Pikes, look out for faint grassy paths to your left. The path for the first of the two is soon after you round it, and leads up to the true summit of the Pikes (NY 413 148); the path for the second, slightly lower and easier to climb, is immediately after the tarn comes into view. Both require short scrambles to the tops.

3 Back on the main path, continue on towards Angle Tarn. The path reaches a junction with a stony track and then passes close to the northern edge of the tarn; drop down off it to reach the water (NY 417 145). Return the way you came, but instead of taking the grassy path back to the summit area, stay on the stony track. This leads back to the junction met earlier, beyond the Pikes. Follow this path to retrace your steps back to Boredale Hause, then pick up the path back to Patterdale (note: be careful not to take the fork left immediately after the Hause, which leads to Hartsop). For a different way down, 300m on from Boredale Hause, at a fork of paths marked by trees, bear left. This drops down towards Patterdale, meeting the path followed earlier beneath the green bench. Drop down to the gate into the narrow road, and follow it back to the village.

Angletarn Pikes

Howtown •

▲ PLACE FELL

• Patterdale

▲ ANGLETARN PIKES

• Hartsop

HIGH STREET ▲

MILES
0   1   2   3   4

from Brothers Water

NATURAL FEATURES

The distinctive double summit of Angletarn Pikes is a familiar feature high above the Patterdale valley: the two sharp peaks arrest attention from a distance and are no less imposing on close acquaintance, being attainable only by rock-scrambling, easy or difficult according to choice of route. The western flank of the fell drops steeply in slopes of bracken to the pleasant strath of the Goldrill Beck; on this side Dubhow Crag and Fall Crag are prominent. More precipitous is the eastern face overlooking the quiet deer sanctuary of Bannerdale, where the great bastion of Heck Crag is a formidable object rarely seen by walkers. The fell is a part of a broad curving ridge that comes down from the High Street watershed and continues to Boredale Hause, beyond which Place Fell terminates it abruptly.

The crowning glory of the Pikes, however, is the tarn from which they are named, cradled in a hollow just below the summit. Its indented shore and islets are features unusual in mountain tarns, and it has for long, and deservedly, been a special attraction for visitors to Patterdale. The charms of Angle Tarn, at all seasons of the year, are manifold: in scenic values it ranks amongst the best of Lakeland tarns.

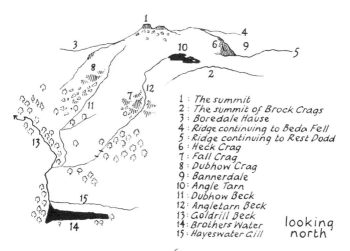

1 : The summit
2 : The summit of Brock Crags
3 : Boredale Hause
4 : Ridge continuing to Beda Fell
5 : Ridge continuing to Rest Dodd
6 : Heck Crag
7 : Fall Crag
8 : Dubhow Crag
9 : Bannerdale
10 : Angle Tarn
11 : Dubhow Beck
12 : Angletarn Beck
13 : Goldrill Beck
14 : Brothers Water
15 : Hayeswater Gill

looking north

169

Red Screes and
Brothers Water
from the top of
Dubhow Beck

Heck Crag
from the
Patterdale-
Martindale path

MAP

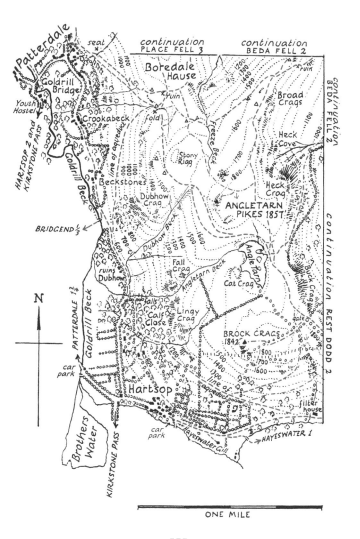

ONE MILE

ASCENT FROM PATTERDALE
1400 feet of ascent : 1¾ miles
Note that this is the initial part of the route to High Street

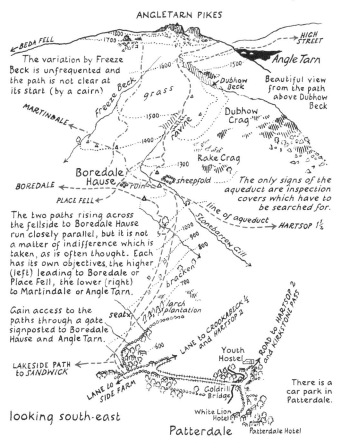

ANGLETARN PIKES

← BEDA FELL

HIGH STREET →

Angle Tarn

The variation by Freeze Beck is unfrequented and the path is not clear at its start (by a cairn)

Freeze Beck

grass

MARTINDALE ←

ravine

Dubhow Beck

Beautiful view from the path above Dubhow Beck

Dubhow Crag

Rake Crag

Boredale Hause

BOREDALE ←

PLACE FELL ←

ruin

sheepfold

The only signs of the aqueduct are inspection covers which have to be searched for.

line of aqueduct

HARTSOP 1½ →

Stonebarrow Gill

The two paths rising across the fellside to Boredale Hause run closely parallel, but it is not a matter of indifference which is taken, as is often thought. Each has its own objectives, the higher (left) leading to Boredale or Place Fell, the lower (right) to Martindale or Angle Tarn.

Gain access to the paths through a gate signposted to Boredale Hause and Angle Tarn.

bracken

seat

larch plantation

LANE to CROOKABECK ¼ and HARTSOP 2

Youth Hostel

ROAD to HARTSOP 2 and KIRKSTONE PASS

LAKESIDE PATH to SANDWICK

LANE to SIDE FARM

Goldrill Bridge

White Lion Hotel

There is a car park in Patterdale.

looking south-east

Patterdale

Patterdale Hotel

This delightful walk should be in the itinerary of all who stay at Patterdale; the climb is pleasant and the views excellent. Combined with a detour to Angle Tarn, it is an easy half-day's excursion.

ASCENT FROM MARTINDALE
1300 feet of ascent : 3½ miles from Martindale Old Church

ANGLETARN PIKES

looking west

Angle Tarn — Buck Crag — 1700 — Heck Crag — 1600 — Heck Cove — Broad Crags — ruin× — Bedafell Knott — BEDA FELL

1600 — 1500 — 1400 — 1300 — 1200 — 1100

bracken — 1500 — 1400 — 1300 — 1200 — bracken — 1100

1000 — 900 — boulder — 1000 — 900 — gate — gate

fold — ruin — 800 — 700

From the foot of Heck Crag there is a beautiful view of Bannerdale Beck meandering through natural vegetation.

Bannerdale Beck — Dale Head

Dale Head farmhouse is interesting architecturally

ROAD TO MARTINDALE CHURCH 1¼

Two routes are illustrated; both are good.
   The valley route, by the wall, is an example of a beautiful and interesting footway falling from favour simply because few now know of it. It ascends the secluded and unfrequented valley of Bannerdale, passes below Heck Crag by a sporting path on steep scree and crosses a low saddle to Angle Tarn, which comes into view suddenly and dramatically: the highlight of the walk. An easy climb (right) leads to the top.
   The more direct way makes use of the path to Patterdale, but turns left when the ridge is gained and keeps to the Bannerdale edge until the summit is close on the right.
   If the return is to be made to Martindale, use the valley route for the ascent (because of the sudden revelation of Angle Tarn, a surprise worth planning) and the ridge route for descent.

THE SUMMIT

The north (main) summit

Angle Tarn from the south summit

   Twin upthrusts of rock, 200 yards apart, give individuality to this unusual summit; the northerly is the higher. Otherwise the top is generally grassy, with an extensive peat bog in a depression.
DESCENTS : Routes of ascent may be reversed. (Note that, to find the Bannerdale valley-path, it is necessary first to descend to Angle Tarn and there cross the low saddle on the left just to the north of a peat gully). *In mist,* there is comfort in knowing that the path for Patterdale is only 100 yards distant down the west slope.

THE VIEW

Principal Fells

Although the view is largely confined by surrounding heights to a five-mile radius it is full of interest. The abrupt summit gives splendid depth and fall to the prospect south-west, where there is a beautiful picture of Brothers Water and Kirkstonefoot. Deepdale, directly below, is especially well seen.

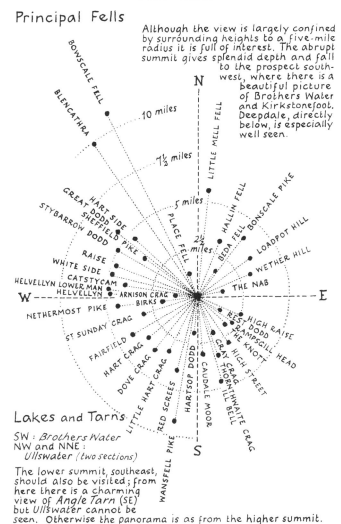

Lakes and Tarns

SW : *Brothers Water*
NW and NNE :
  Ullswater (two sections)

The lower summit, southeast, should also be visited; from here there is a charming view of *Angle Tarn* (SE) but *Ullswater* cannot be seen. Otherwise the panorama is as from the higher summit.

RIDGE ROUTES

To BEDA FELL, 1670' : 2 miles
NE, then N and NE
*Main depression at 1450'
and several minor depressions*
300 feet of ascent

An easy walk, the latter part being dull.
Aim for the high knoll north-east, where
an interesting path leads down a
narrowing shoulder (good views of
Bannerdale and Heck Crag here).
The Patterdale-Martindale path
is crossed as it tops the ridge.
Beyond, the walk becomes
uninteresting. *Beda Fell is
dangerous in mist, having
precipitous crags on the
eastern flank, and the
ridge is ill-defined
beyond the summit.*

The Patterdale-Martindale path is an easy way of escape in bad weather; there is a cairn at the cross-paths.

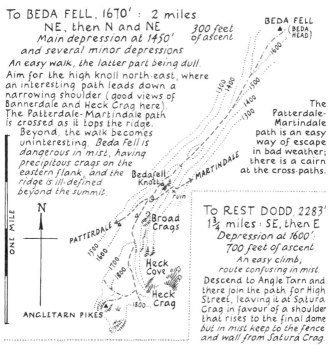

To REST DODD, 2283'
1¾ miles : SE, then E
*Depression at 1600'.
700 feet of ascent.*

*An easy climb;
route confusing in mist.*
Descend to Angle Tarn and
there join the path for High
Street, leaving it at Satura
Crag in favour of a shoulder
that rises to the final dome
*but in mist keep to the fence
and wall from Satura Crag.*

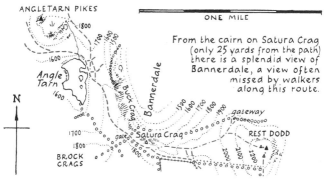

From the cairn on Satura Crag (only 25 yards from the path) there is a splendid view of Bannerdale, a view often missed by walkers along this route.

14 Catbells
from Keswick launch or Hawse End

For many Lake District walkers, Catbells is where it all began. One of the classic family fells, its shape is instantly recognisable, with broad and well-worn paths that have carried generations up to their first Lakeland summit, from which there are wonderful views over the grander peaks and down to Derwent Water. Its pretty slopes are where Beatrix Potter made Mrs Tiggy-Winkle's home in her children's tales, and even its name – probably derived from cat bield, or the shelter or den of the wild cat – stirs the imagination. As Wainwright puts it in his notes: 'Catbells is one of the great favourites, a family fell where grandmothers and infants can climb the heights together: a place beloved.'

This route up Catbells follows Wainwright's suggestion of adding in a ferry ride over Derwent Water from Keswick. It requires a little advance planning to coincide with departures from the landing stages at the start and finish, but the short trip over the lake is a fine prelude to the walk, and any time waiting for the ferry service at Keswick or Hawse End can be spent with a picnic or skimming stones from the shore. The climb from Hawse End is steady and over mostly easy paths, while the descent reverses Wainwright's route from Grange, then picks up the path of the long-distance Allerdale Ramble to return to Hawse End and the ferry.

Most families will be able to manage the walk over the course of a leisurely day, though as Wainwright points out, Catbells is not without its challenges. Take care with children as you go, as the drop down is steep in places – as is the climb itself at times, and a succession of 'false' summits on the way up means younger ones might need some cajoling. There are also a couple of short scrambles up to the rocky summit, though these do help to give young walkers a great sense of achievement on reaching the top proper.

To climb Catbells without the ferry ride, start the walk at Hawse End and pick up the directions from point 2. To shorten the walk by about 1½ miles more, simply return the way you came up rather than pressing on to Hause Gate. To extend it, continue over the splendid ridge for about 1½ miles, past Hause Gate and on to Maiden Moor.

From *Book Six: The North Western Fells*

Distance 4½ miles (7.2km)

Ascent 1,250 feet (380m)

Start and finish point The ferry landing stages at Keswick (NY 264 227) or the parking place at Hawse End (NY 247 212)

Ordnance Survey maps Explorer OL4; Landranger 90

Getting there

The landing stages at Keswick are at the south end of the town, a short stroll from the centre. Follow the signposts out of town, passing the theatre before reaching the ferry ticket kiosk and landing stages at the lake. The landing stages and theatre share an adjacent pay-and-display car park if you are arriving by car. Ferries run from the landing stages to Hawse End every hour in the summer, between about 9.45am and 4.30pm, and return at the same frequency. Between mid-November and mid-March the service is much reduced. Check times in advance to plan your day (017687 72263, www.keswick-launch.co.uk). The journey time is about 10 minutes.

If you wish to cut out the ferry ride and make straight for Catbells, parking is available off the road a little way in from the lake by Hawse End. To reach it from Keswick, make for Portinscale and then take the minor road that follows the lake's shore down to Hawse End. The spaces fill up quickly in the summer; there is further parking a short drive on towards Skelgill.

Both Keswick and Hawse End are served by buses. Services to Keswick include the 555 from Kendal, Windermere and

Ambleside; the 554 from Carlisle and Wigton; the X4 and X5 from Cockermouth and Penrith and places between; and the 78 from Borrowdale. By train, make for Penrith and take the X4 or X5 bus. Hawse End can be reached from Keswick or Buttermere on the 77 bus, which runs about four times a day in a loop in either direction from early April to early November. Take the clockwise service. It drops off by the parking spaces.

Facilities, food and drink

The kiosk by the landing stages at Keswick sells drinks and snacks, and there are public toilets in the adjacent car park. The town itself has plenty of places to make up a picnic for the walk, including a large Booths supermarket (017687 73518, www. booths.co.uk). Hawse End has no shop or facilities, so stock up in Keswick first.

Good cafés in Keswick include the Lakeland Pedlar by the Bell Close car park (017687 74492, www.lakelandpedlar.co.uk) and Abraham's on the top floor of the famous George Fisher outdoor equipment shop on Borrowdale Road (017687 72178, www. georgefisher.co.uk). Its website has a webcam if you want to check the weather in Keswick before setting out. Family-friendly pubs include The Twa Dogs Inn on Penrith Road (017687 72599, www. twadogs.co.uk) and The Dog & Gun on Lake Road (017687 73463).

Keswick has plenty of diversions for children, including the Pencil Museum on Main Street (017687 73626, www. pencilmuseum.co.uk) and the Puzzling Place, an imaginative collection of puzzles, curiosities and optical illusions on Museum Square (017687 75102, www.puzzlingplace. co.uk). There is a swimming pool above the town on Station Road (017687 72760, www.carlisleleisure.com) and a large playground and park just below it. The Theatre by the Lake by the landing stages is highly recommended and often has activities for children in the school holidays (017687 74411, www.theatrebythelake.co.uk). For lots more ideas for things to do in Keswick, call into the Tourist Information Centre in the Moot Hall on Market Square (017687 72645).

Directions

1 Buy your tickets from the kiosk and take the ferry from the landing stages in the anti-clockwise direction. The journey around the lake to Hawse End takes about ten minutes. From the landing stage at Hawse End, walk away from the lake to reach a small wooden gate followed by a bridge. Rise up through the wood to reach a narrow road, and turn right. After about 60m, turn left off the road and climb up a footpath by a wall, signposted for Catbells and Newlands valley. This rises up to another narrow road. Continue ahead up it, soon crossing a cattle-grid.

2 (If you are starting the walk at Hawse End, turn right up the road from the parking spaces.) Where the road bends back on itself in a hairpin, leave it to step onto the hillside via some stone steps, the way indicated by a signpost for Catbells summit. The path is now very clear for about 1 mile as you ascend Catbells. Just before the first of a succession of mini summits, by a memorial tablet identified by Wainwright in his notes, is a short scramble over rock. Over more intermediary peaks and depressions, the path leads up to the summit of Catbells (NY 244 199).

3 Continue on over the ridge for about ½ mile, until you reach a crossroads of paths called Hause Gate (NY 244 192). Here turn left to descend down some stone steps, with intermittent fencing alongside to prevent erosion. Further down, at another junction of paths, turn left down more stone steps in the direction of the lake.

4 Soon meet another path that is sturdier and flatter. Turn left along it, now running in parallel with the lake. Eventually the path converges with a minor road beneath it. Bear left around the base of Catbells, and just before you reach the cattle-grid crossed earlier, look for a turn to the right that leads you down to the path through the woods, back to the landing stage at Hawse End.

Catbells

1481'

Cat Bells
(two words)
on Ordnance maps

from Derwent Water

Portinscale
Keswick

Stair

▲ CATBELLS
Little Town
▲ MAIDEN MOOR
Grange

MILES

0   1   2   3   4

from the Portinscale path

NATURAL FEATURES

Catbells is one of the great favourites, a family fell where grandmothers and infants can climb the heights together, a place beloved. Its popularity is well deserved: its shapely topknot attracts the eye, offering a steep but obviously simple scramble to the small summit; its slopes are smooth, sunny and sleek; its position overlooking Derwent Water is superb. Moreover, for stronger walkers it is the first step on a glorious ridge that bounds Borrowdale on the west throughout its length with Newlands down on the other side. There is beauty everywhere — and nothing but beauty. Its ascent from Keswick may conveniently, in the holiday season, be coupled with a sail on the lake, making the expedition rewarding out of all proportion to the small effort needed. Even the name has a magic challenge.

Yet this fell is not quite so innocuous as is usually thought, and grandmothers and infants should have a care as they romp around. There are some natural hazards in the form of a line of crags that starts at the summit and slants down to Newlands, and steep outcrops elsewhere. More dangerous are the levels and open shafts that pierce the fell on both flanks: the once-prosperous Yewthwaite Mine despoils a wide area in the combe above Little Town in Newlands, to the east the debris of the ill-starred Brandley Mine is lapped by the water of the lake, and the workings of the Old Brandley Mine, high on the side of the fell at Skelgill Bank, are in view on the ascent of the ridge from the north. A tragic death in one of the open Yewthwaite shafts in 1962 serves as a warning.

Words cannot adequately describe the rare charm of Catbells, nor its ravishing view. But no publicity is necessary: its mere presence in the Derwent Water scene is enough. It has a bold 'come hither' look that compels one's steps, and no suitor ever returns disappointed, but only looking back often. It has only to be seen from Friar's Crag — and a spell is cast. No Keswick holiday is consummated without a visit to Catbells.

from Yewthwaite Comb

Crags and Caverns of Catbells

left: The crags of Mart Bield, below the summit on the Newlands side of the fell

right: A dangerous hole at Yewthwaite Mine. At the end of a rock cutting the adit suggests a level (horizontal tunnel) but in fact is the opening of a vertical shaft.

below: Workings at the Old Brandley Mine. A shaft with twin entrances, overhung by a tree, *left*, and a nearby level, *right*.

MAP

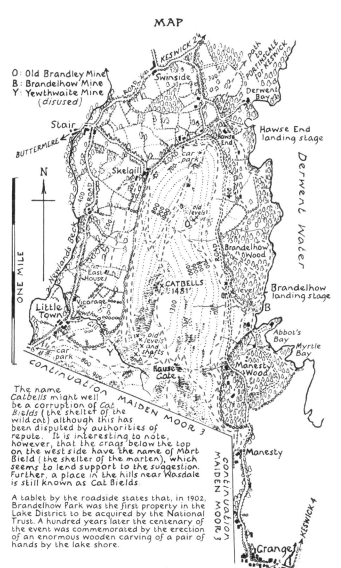

O: Old Brandley Mine
B: Brandelhow Mine
Y: Yewthwaite Mine
    (disused)

The name Catbells might well be a corruption of *Cat Bields* (the shelter of the wild cat) although this has been disputed by authorities of repute. It is interesting to note, however, that the crags below the top on the west side have the name of *Mart Bield* (the shelter of the marten), which seems to lend support to the suggestion. Further, a place in the hills near Wasdale is still known as *Cat Bields*.

A tablet by the roadside states that, in 1902, Brandelhow Park was the first property in the Lake District to be acquired by the National Trust. A hundred years later the centenary of the event was commemorated by the erection of an enormous wooden carving of a pair of hands by the lake shore.

ASCENT FROM HAWSE END
1250 feet of ascent : 1½ miles

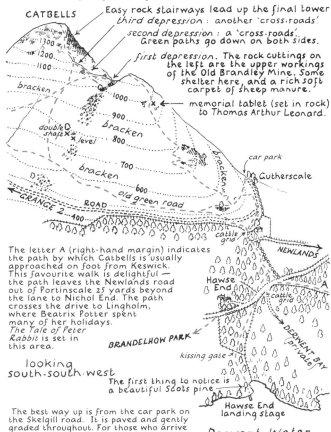

CATBELLS

Easy rock stairways lead up the final tower
third depression : another 'cross-roads'

second depression : a 'cross-roads'.
Green paths go down on both sides.

first depression. The rock cuttings on
the left are the upper workings
of the Old Brandley Mine. Some
shelter here, and a rich soft
carpet of sheep manure.

1300
1200
1100

bracken

1000
900

memorial tablet (set in rock)
to Thomas Arthur Leonard.

double
shaft
level

bracken
800

700

bracken

car park

600

Gutherscale

old green road

ROAD

GRANGE 2

400

cattle grid

NEWLANDS

The letter A (right-hand margin) indicates
the path by which Catbells is usually
approached on foot from Keswick.
This favourite walk is delightful —
the path leaves the Newlands road
out of Portinscale 25 yards beyond
the lane to Nichol End. The path
crosses the drive to Lingholm,
where Beatrix Potter spent
many of her holidays.
*The Tale of Peter
Rabbit* is set in
this area.

Hawse
End

cattle grid

A

DERWENT BAY (private)

looking
south·south·west

BRANDELHOW PARK

kissing gate

The first thing to notice is
a beautiful Scots pine

The best way up is from the car park on
the Skelgill road. It is paved and gently
graded throughout. For those who arrive
by bus or on foot an alternative path
leaves from the road junction and curves
left to join the path from the car park.

Woodford's Path:
*This series of zigzags was engineered
by a Sir John Woodford, who lived near,
and his name deserves to be remembered
by those who use his enchanting stairway.
It starts 80 yards along the old green road.*

Hawse End
landing stage

Derwent Water

Hawse End is served
by motor·launch from
Keswick.

One of the very best
of the shorter climbs.
A truly lovely walk.

184

ASCENT FROM GRANGE
1250 feet of ascent : 2 miles

Of course there is no gate at Hause Gate, just as there is no door at Mickledoor. 'Gate' and 'door' are local geographical terms for a way or opening through the hills or across a ridge. 'Hause' is another good Lakeland name for a pass. 'Hause Gate' is therefore really a tautological name. 'Hawse End' (with a 'w') is not a misspelling, 'hause' being inappropriate to the place.

Except for the zigzags below Hause Gate, the whole climb is set at an easy gradient, making it ideal for a gentle stroll on a fine evening after a big meal. The view opens beautifully as height is gained on a wide grass path, the start of which, near Manesty Farm, is the old road to Hawse End, now part of the long-distance footpath, the Allerdale Ramble.

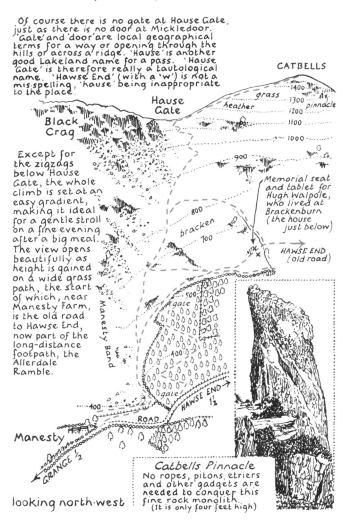

CATBELLS

1400 · grass · pinnacle
1300
1200 · heather
1100
1000
900
800 · bracken · 700
500 · gate
400 · gate

Hause Gate

Black Crag

Memorial seat and tablet for Hugh Walpole, who lived at Brackenburn (the house just below)

HAWSE END (old road)

HAWSE END → 1½

Manesty Band

Manesty

ROAD

← GRANGE ½

looking north-west

Catbells Pinnacle
No ropes, pitons, etriers and other gadgets are needed to conquer this fine rock monolith.
(It is only four feet high)

ASCENT FROM NEWLANDS

via SKELGILL
*1200 feet of ascent : 1½ miles
from Stair*

via LITTLE TOWN
*950 feet of ascent : 1¼ miles
from Little Town*

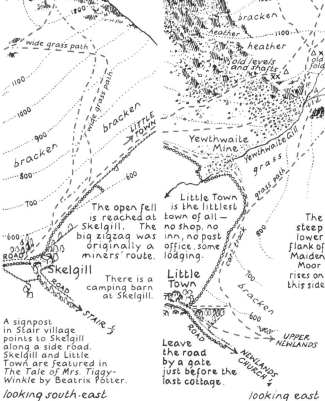

CATBELLS

CATBELLS

Hause Gate

1300

1200

bracken

heather

1100

heather

old levels
and shafts

old
fold

wide grass path

1100

wide grass path

1000

bracken

LITTLE
TOWN

900

bracken

Yewthwaite
Mine

Yewthwaite Gill

grass

800

600

grass path

700

600

600

700

600

bracken

600

UPPER
NEWLANDS

The open fell
is reached at
Skelgill. The
big zigzag was
originally a
miners' route.

There is a
camping barn
at Skelgill.

Little Town
is the littlest
town of all —
no shop, no
inn, no post
office, some
lodging.

The
steep
lower
flank of
Maiden
Moor
rises on
this side

ROAD

Skelgill

ROAD

STAIR ⅓

Little
Town

cart track

ROAD

NEWLANDS
CHURCH ¾

A signpost
in Stair village
points to Skelgill
along a side road.
Skelgill and Little
Town are featured in
*The Tale of Mrs. Tiggy-
Winkle* by Beatrix Potter.

Leave
the road
by a gate
just before the
last cottage.

looking south-east

looking east

Up one way and down the other is a nice idea.

THE SUMMIT

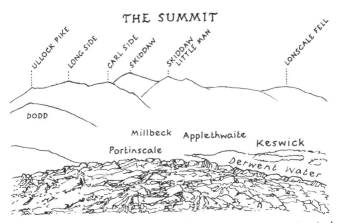

ULLOCK PIKE · LONG SIDE · CARL SIDE · SKIDDAW · SKIDDAW LITTLE MAN · LONSCALE FELL

DODD

Millbeck · Applethwaite · Keswick

Portinscale

Derwent Water

The summit, which has no cairn, is a small platform of naked rock, light brown in colour and seamed and pitted with many tiny hollows and crevices that collect and hold rainwater—so that, long after the skies have cleared, glittering diamonds adorn the crown. Almost all the native vegetation has been scoured away by the varied footgear of countless visitors; so popular is this fine viewpoint that often it is difficult to find a vacant perch. In summer this is not a place to seek quietness. DESCENTS: Leave the top only by the ridge; lower down there is a wealth of choice. Keep clear of the craggy Newlands face.

RIDGE ROUTE

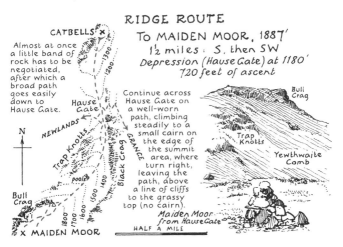

TO MAIDEN MOOR, 1887'
1½ miles : S, then SW
Depression (Hause Gate) at 1180'
720 feet of ascent

CATBELLS X

Almost at once a little band of rock has to be negotiated, after which a broad path goes easily down to Hause Gate.

Hause Gate

NEWLANDS

Trap Knotts

pools

Black Crag

GRANGE

Bull Crag

X MAIDEN MOOR

N

1300 · 1200 · 1400 · 1500 · 1600 · 1700 · 1800

Continue across Hause Gate on a well-worn path, climbing steadily to a small cairn on the edge of the summit area, where turn right, leaving the path, above a line of cliffs to the grassy top (no cairn).

Bull Crag

Trap Knotts

Yewthwaite Comb

Maiden Moor from Hause Gate

HALF A MILE

THE VIEW

Scenes of great beauty unfold on all sides, and they are scenes in depth to a degree not usual, the narrow summit permitting downward views of Borrowdale and Newlands within a few paces. Nearby valley and lake attract the eye more than the distant mountain surround, although Hindscarth and Robinson are particularly prominent at the head of Newlands and Causey Pike towers up almost grotesquely directly opposite. On this side the hamlet of Little Town is well seen down below, a charming picture, but it is to Derwent Water and mid-Borrowdale that the captivated gaze returns again and again.

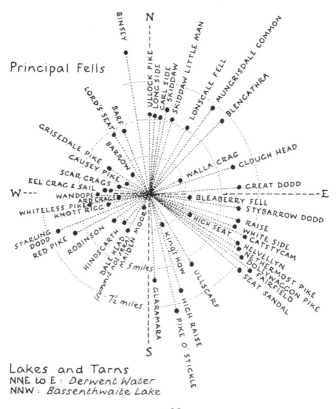

Principal Fells

Lakes and Tarns
NNE to E : Derwent Water
NNW : Bassenthwaite Lake

Hindscarth and Robinson from Catbells

15 Low Fell
from Loweswater

Rising out of the village and lake of Loweswater, in the far north western corner of the Lake District National Park, is Low Fell. This part of the Lakes is well off the beaten track, and it can only be its extremity that means this fell is less walked than most of the other fells in this book. 'The lesser heights and foothills of Lakeland, especially those on the fringe, are too much neglected in favour of the greater mountains, yet many of these unsought and unfashionable little hills are completely charming,' says Wainwright in his notes. 'In this category is Low Fell.'

Mellbreak, covered in Chapter 12 of this book, is another fine walk from Loweswater, but no excuse is needed for including another from the same village – and this one has the extra challenge of a second fell. As Wainwright notes, Low Fell is much more than a single top, strung out along a ridge and criss-crossed by fences. This walk creates a circular route around and over it, starting with a long rise out of the village that gets steadily closer to the lake before leaving it on an old mining track and striking out on to the fell. First up is Darling Fell, not covered separately by Wainwright but named as a summit in its own right on Ordnance Survey maps, before a drop and a second climb leads on to Low Fell proper.

The two peaks come in quick succession, and despite their modest heights they will present children with a good challenge that gets young legs ready for bigger climbs elsewhere. And once up on top, Low Fell is a wonderful place to be, supremely peaceful and picturesque. It is also a fell that can be explored and returned to often, with plenty of vantage and resting points and views that change with the seasons but are always superb, especially over the lakes and fells to the south. Or as Wainwright puts it: 'The view is of classical beauty, an inspired and inspiring vision of loveliness that has escaped the publicity of picture postcards and poets' sonnets, a scene of lakes and mountains arranged to perfection.' That has to be worth a walk to see.

From *Book Seven: The Western Fells*

Distance 4 miles (6.4km)

Ascent 1,550 feet (470m)

Start and finish point The Kirkstile Inn in Loweswater (NY 141 209)

Ordnance Survey maps Explorer OL4; Landranger 89

Getting there

Cars can be parked at the Kirkstile Inn if you eat, drink or stay at the pub before or after. There is roadside parking around the village, but position cars on the verges with care. More spaces can be found near the start of the walk along the lakeside road, or by the end of it at the village's telephone box, though they fill up quickly. You can also park at Waterend at the northern tip of Loweswater lake; walk back towards the village from here, and look for the track turn-off in the directions after a little less than 1 mile.

No buses pass through the village, but the 77 service is just over 1 mile away as it makes its way down the B5289 between Lorton and Buttermere. There are four services a day in both directions around a circular route from Keswick from early April to early November; the anti-clockwise one will get you there quicker. Ask to be dropped in Lanthwaite.

Facilities, food and drink

The Kirkstile Inn is a friendly and traditional Lakeland pub, with good food and local beers and a family-friendly room and terrace by the river (01900 85219, www.kirkstile.com). There are no shops in or around Loweswater, but New House Farm near Brackenthwaite has the Barn Tearooms (07841 159818, www.newhouse-farm.com) and Lorton has the Wheatsheaf Inn (01900 85199, www.wheatsheafinnlorton.co.uk).

For more choice of eating and drinking, head to Buttermere to the south or Cockermouth to the north. For more activities, Loweswater and Crummock Water both offer splendid lakeside walks and paddling, and Whinlatter Forest to the north east has a host of things to do including forest trails, bike hire, high-wire adventure lines, picnic spots, café and playgrounds (017687 78469, www.visitlakelandforests.co.uk).

Directions

1 Turn left out of the car park by the Kirkstile Inn and up the road. At a T-junction, turn left to continue rising and ignore other side-roads in quick succession on the right and left. The road is quiet and much used by walkers and cyclists, but take care. It passes a series of fine Lakeland houses and, beyond the last of them, an old pinfold – a sort of jail for errant livestock for which a constable-style pinder would charge to return to their owner; a National Trust sign explains more. Soon after the pinfold, and just under 1 mile in all from Loweswater, branch right off the road onto a track, signposted for Mosser (NY 128 218). After just over 1/3 mile on this, branch off to the right over a stile in a fence, signposted for Foulsyke (note that it is not the first path off to the right, by a wooden bench, but the second, easily obscured by branches; NY 124 224).

2 Over the stile, bear left and uphill, following the line of a fence. Don't forget to look both back for views over the lake and left across to Askill Knott. Follow the fence as it bends right at a right-angle, but further up, where it right-angles to the left, leave it to continue walking in the same direction. After crossing a stile in a fence, the path leads on to a cairn that marks the highest point of Darling Fell (NY 130 225). The area around here, with grassy expanses and fine views over lakes and fells, is a good spot for a picnic and rest.

3 Continue on the grassy path ahead, soon picking up another fence on your left. This descends to a depression and crosses a fell stream, Crabtree Beck, before rising up Low Fell; it looks dauntingly steep from the other side but is much easier in practice. After most of the climbing is done, look out for a stile in the fence on the left, and cross it for a short stretch up to the northern summit of Low Fell; the cairn soon comes into view (NY 137 226). See Wainwright's notes on the uncertainty about the highest point.

4 Return to the stile in the fence, but do not cross it and instead turn left to drop down. The slopes are covered with heather at first and then bracken, and the drop is steep, but the fence is your guide and safety rail throughout. At a height of about 700 feet, look for a stile in the fence on your right. Do not cross it, but instead turn left on the path from it to traverse the hillside for just over 100m until, immediately after a stream, it turns right down between trees and through bracken. It now crosses a wall by a stile, then drops further to a fence and turns right to cross a small stream (NY 143 224).

5 The path hugs a fence on the left and crosses a stile to pass through a wood, the level and shade welcome after all the climbing earlier. Follow the fence to the far tip of the wood, crossing another stile a third of the way through, then exit via a stile and wooden gate to pick up a grassy track to two wooden gates, the second of which accesses a road (NY 142 215). Turn left, but after 50m carefully cross and leave the road to the right through another gate, the way indicated by a public footpath signpost. After ¼ mile the path reaches a gate on to a road. Turn right and then first left for the Kirkstile Inn.

Low Fell

1352'

from Lanthwaite Hill

The lesser heights and foothills of Lakeland, especially those on the fringe, are too much neglected in favour of the greater mountains, yet many of these unsought and unfashionable little hills are completely charming. In this category is Low Fell, north of Loweswater and west of the Vale of Lorton. It has many tops, uniformly around 1350 feet, rising from a ridge. The most southerly eminence has the main cairn and a perfectly composed view of mountain and lake scenery, a connoisseur's piece.

Low Fell and Fellbarrow together form a separate range, a final upthrust of land between Lakeland and the sea. The underlying rock is slate, and the hills exhibit smooth rounded slopes in conformity to pattern; but they deny conformity to the lake of Loweswater, forcing its issuing stream, by a freak of contours, to flow inland, away from the sea, in compliance with the inexorable natural law that water always obeys.

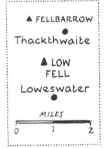

▲ FELLBARROW

● Thackthwaite

▲ LOW FELL

Loweswater ●

MILES

0   1   2

MAP

continuation FELLBARROW 3·4

MOSSER

This lane is permanently flooded to a depth of 12"

Smithy Fell

old quarry

Thackthwaite

Watching Crag

Sourfoot Fell

Loftbarrow

Wilderness Wood

Red How

Thackthwaite Leys Wood

Latterhead

Askill Knott

LAMPLUGH MOCKERKIN

stile

Darling Fell

old fold

stile

Crabtree Beck

LOW FELL 1352

stile

Oak Bank

River Cocker

Loweswater

Scale Hill

car park

700

Foulsyke

Crabtreebeck

Thrushbank

Highcross

Dub Beck

ROAD

N

ONE MILE

Hall

Church

Inn

Loweswater (also known as Kirkstile)

ROAD

COCKERMOUTH

ROAD

Fellwalkers in Lakeland are privileged by complete freedom to wander on the hills (by the grace of owners and tenants until 2005, and now as of right) and rarely meet obstructions to progress other than natural obstacles. The stone walls and wire fences above the intakes are not generally maintained and often ruinous.

This is not the position, however, on Low Fell and the neighbouring Fellbarrow, and it is surprising to find here that, although some fences have gone most of them are kept in tight repair. Unusual, too, is the neat parcelling of the upland pastures into enclosed allotments. Sheep normally live their lives on the heaf they were brought up on, convinced there's no place like home, and need no fences to persuade them to stay. It seems that the fences must therefore define the individual grazing rights of several farmers. It is not unusual for farmers to have rights in common, but it is unusual to separate their holdings so distinctly on the felltops.

ASCENT FROM LOWESWATER
1050 feet of ascent : 2 miles (direct route)
1350 feet of ascent : 3 miles (via Darling Fell)

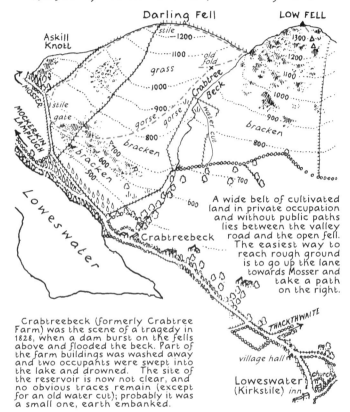

A wide belt of cultivated land in private occupation and without public paths lies between the valley road and the open fell. The easiest way to reach rough ground is to go up the lane towards Mosser and take a path on the right.

Crabtreebeck (formerly Crabtree Farm) was the scene of a tragedy in 1828, when a dam burst on the fells above and flooded the beck. Part of the farm buildings was washed away and two occupants were swept into the lake and drowned. The site of the reservoir is now not clear, and no obvious traces remain (except for an old water cut); probably it was a small one, earth embanked.

Follow the Mosser lane for a third of a mile, leaving at a gate recessed on the right. The path from here to the old fold is very difficult to follow, particularly where it passes through gorse bushes. If the path is lost aim for the fold.
To include Darling Fell in the walk continue up the Mosser lane beyond the gate for a hundred yards and turn right at a stile and signpost. This route is easy to follow, but there is a considerable depression between Darling Fell and Low Fell.

Wait for a bright clear day.   Don't forget the camera.

ASCENT FROM THACKTHWAITE
1250 feet of ascent : 2 miles

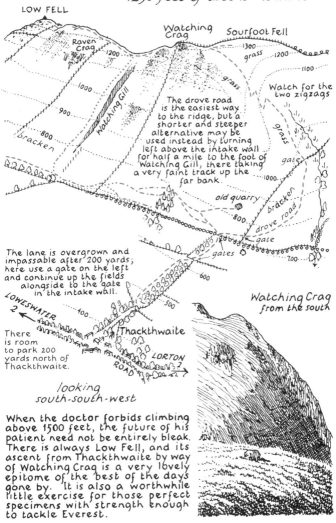

LOW FELL

Raven Crag

Watching Crag

Sourfoot Fell

1300

1200

grass

1200

1100

1000

Watch for the two zigzags

grass

900

Watching Gill

800

bracken

The drove road is the easiest way to the ridge, but a shorter and steeper alternative may be used instead by turning left above the intake wall for half a mile to the foot of Watching Gill, there taking a very faint track up the far bank.

old quarry

800

1000

bracken

gate

drove road

800

gate

gates

700

600

The lane is overgrown and impassable after 200 yards; here use a gate on the left and continue up the fields alongside to the gate in the intake wall.

100

LOWESWATER 2

500

There is room to park 200 yards north of Thackthwaite.

Thackthwaite

LORTON 2

ROAD

looking south-south-west

Watching Crag *from the south*

When the doctor forbids climbing above 1500 feet, the future of his patient need not be entirely bleak. There is always Low Fell, and its ascent from Thackthwaite by way of Watching Crag is a very lovely epitome of the best of the days gone by. It is also a worthwhile little exercise for those perfect specimens with strength enough to tackle Everest.

197

THE SUMMIT

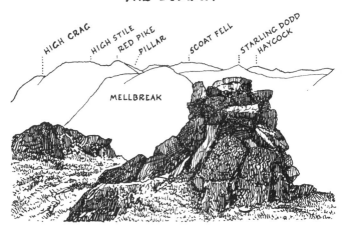

HIGH CRAG
HIGH STILE
RED PIKE
PILLAR
SCOAT FELL
STARLING DODD
HAYCOCK

MELLBREAK

The biggest cairn is on the southern eminence, which is treated as the summit in this book, but the smooth north top appears to be slightly higher. This is confirmed by the 2008 edition of the 2½" map, which gives the altitudes as 1352' and 1388' respectively. This means that the column at 1363' on the more massive Fellbarrow is not the highest point on the range, as was once thought. Two cairns 100 and 120 yards southeast of the main cairn indicate better viewpoints for the Loweswater valley.

DESCENTS : For Foulsyke head north and follow the fence steeply down to a horizontal path leading to a stile in the intake wall. The steepness may be avoided by taking the longer route to Thackthwaite. For Crabtreebeck follow the ridge to the north and look for a path on the left leading to a fence. Follow the fence down to Crabtree Beck and turn left to a sheepfold. Beyond here the route becomes confusing, and it is easier to use the longer route over Darling How.

GRASMOOR

LOW FELL
(south top)

*Cairn on
Darling Fell*

*Cairn on the north top
(now just
a pile of
stones)*

The cairn on Darling Fell marks the end of the ridge and not the highest point. The highest point is situated forty yards east of the fence coming up from the Mosser lane.

THE VIEW

Southeast the view is of classical beauty, an inspired and inspiring vision of loveliness that has escaped the publicity of picture postcards and poets' sonnets, a scene of lakes and mountains arranged to perfection. The grouping of fells above Mosedale is also attractively presented, with Pillar an unexpected absentee, only a small section of its western shoulder being seen behind Red Pike. Grasmoor is a tremendous object.

Westwards is the sea.

Principal Fells

The diagram is based on the view from the south top.

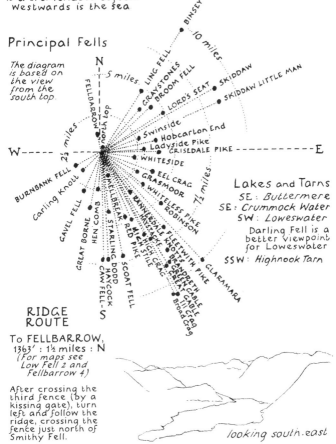

Lakes and Tarns

SE: *Buttermere*
SE: *Crummock Water*
SW: *Loweswater*

Darling Fell is a better viewpoint for Loweswater

SSW: *Highnook Tarn*

RIDGE ROUTE

To FELLBARROW, 1363' : 1½ miles : N
(For maps see Low Fell 2 and Fellbarrow 4)

After crossing the third fence (by a kissing gate), turn left and follow the ridge, crossing the fence just north of Smithy Fell.

looking south-east

16 Walla Crag
from Keswick

Wainwright called Walla Crag 'a brief but excellent insight into the joys of fell-walking' – and as usual he was right. It is an ideal introduction to the Lake District for young or reluctant walkers alike, offering the high fells in miniature: steep enough to present a challenge but gentle enough for the end, or at least the next resting point, never to be far away.

This is one of the handful of popular family walks from the tourist hotspot of Keswick, easily reached from the town without the need for those staying there to drive anywhere before lacing up their boots. Its popularity among families means you are unlikely to be alone on this walk whatever the time of year – though it is not half as busy as the streets of Keswick itself, which are quickly left behind on this route. Like so many of the most walked Lakeland fells, Walla Crag has become something a victim of its own success, but that is no reason to miss it. Or as Wainwright warns in his notes: 'No excuse is good enough.'

As he also points out, the view of Walla Crag from below is of a dramatic, green and rocky top, but the paths up to it from Keswick are fairly easy all the way. The route outlined here closely follows Wainwright's suggested ascent from the town, while for variety the descent detours through a quiet wood before rejoining the original path back to the town.

The combination of fabulous views of Derwent Water and plentiful expanses of flat space makes Walla Crag the ideal place for a leisurely picnic before coming down again, so take your time over the walk if you can. If you have been revived by your lunch and want to extend things into something more strenuous, you could continue for just over a mile south east to the summit of Bleaberry Fell, the subject of another chapter in the third book of Wainwright's *Pictorial Guides* – though Walla Crag comfortably merits both a separate listing and a walk in its own right.

From *Book Three: The Central Fells*

Distance 5 miles (8km)

Ascent 1,000 feet (300m)

Start and finish point The Moot Hall and Tourist Information Centre in Keswick's Market Square (NY 266 234)

Ordnance Survey maps Explorer OL4; Landranger 89 or 90

Getting there

Keswick is just off both the A591 and the A66, connecting to junction 40 of the M6. There are plenty of car parks in town within a short walk of the starting point, though they get very busy during the summer months and none are cheap. Try the Central, Bell Close or Otley Road car parks. Street parking is restricted by a disc system. Before setting out from the starting point at the Moot Hall, glance up at the unusual one-handed clock in its tower.

Keswick is very well served by buses, including from Windermere, Ambleside and the south by the 555 service and from the west and east by the X4 and X5. The nearest train station is Penrith on the west coast mainline, 17 miles away. The X4 or X5 bus connects it to Keswick.

Facilities, food and drink

Wherever you are in Keswick, you will not have to walk far for refreshments. This is a town dedicated to walkers and tourists, crammed with B&Bs, cafés and outdoor equipment shops. For a cup of tea and something to eat, recommended options include Abraham's Tea Room at the top of the George Fisher outdoor shop on Borrowdale Road (017687 72178, www.georgefisher.co.uk). It is named after two brothers, famous Lakeland photographers, and there are great views if you can get a seat by the window, though pram or buggy pushers will find the steps up to it difficult.

Elsewhere in Keswick, the Lakeland Pedlar on Henderson's Yard (017687 74492, www.lakelandpedlar. co.uk) and the Wild Strawberry on Main Street (017687 74399) are good cafés offering light meals as well as tea and cakes. Keswick's best pubs include the nicely old fashioned Dog & Gun on Lake Road (017687 73463). On a sunny day, you could put together a picnic for Walla Crag from one of the cafés or Booths supermarket on Tithebarne Road (017687 73518, www.booths.co.uk).

The excellent Tourist Information Centre at the starting point of this walk can provide advice on accommodation and entertainments if you are seeking to stay in Keswick for a while. The town has several family-friendly museums that can all provide a diverting few hours before or after this walk, including the Pencil Museum (017687 73626, www. pencilmuseum.co.uk) and the Mining Museum (017687 80055, www.keswickminingmuseum.co.uk). There are two good parks too: Hope Park, with miniature golf; and Fitz Park, with a large playground.

Directions

1 Exit the Market Square on Ambleside Road, very quickly leaving the bustle of the town centre behind. You soon pass St John's Church on your right. About 400m further on, turn right on to Springs Road. Follow this road for about ½ mile, at which point it peters out by a bridge, stream and farm (NY 276 226). Continue along the track ahead, keeping to the right of some farm buildings and entering a wood through a gate. The track rises along the beck at first, then bends right at a fork, signposted for Rakefoot Farm and Walla Crag, and continues to climb. Continue past a large TV mast, then ignore a path joining from the right. Reach a small gate, which takes you back into the edge of the wood,

soon descending to a footbridge. Cross, and rise up on the other side of the beck to a road (NY 283 222).

2 Turn right up the road towards Rakefoot Farm. At a fork, follow the right-hand lane, signposted for Walla Crag. Where the road runs out, cross the footbridge to your right and take the right of two paths forward, again signposted for Walla Crag, to climb to a gate by a wall corner. Follow the path with the wall to your right, ignoring the side-path over to the left. It sticks closely to the wall for the remainder of the way to the top of Walla Crag, and it is a rather steep slog at first – but efforts are soon rewarded with fine views back down over Keswick and Derwent Water. After about ¾ mile the summit area is reached, and a stile in the wall leads through bracken to the cairn – though the drops to the right can be a little hair-raising if you are with small children, so it might be better to wait for the second stile further along the wall, which leads a few steps straight to the cairn (NY 277 213). There are more tremendous views of the lake and fells from here.

3 From the cairn, continue along the path to re-cross the wall that you followed to the top. With this again on your right as a guide, descend, steeply and through several small gates. The path soon picks up Cat Gill and its waterfall close by, and then enters a wood called Great Wood. Continue to wind down, reaching a footbridge on your left. Do not cross it, but instead bear right, going further into the wood. At a crossroads of paths in a dip, turn right and climb. The clear track now leads you through the wood, with Walla Crag above to your right. After just over 1 mile, the track leaves the wood and soon after reaches a junction with another (NY 280 223). Turn left. This is the path followed earlier, and it descends past the TV mast and back down to the track and Springs Road. Back on Ambleside Road, turn left for the Moot Hall.

Walla Crag

1243'

'Wallow Crag'
on old editions
of Ordnance
Survey maps

from Falcon Crag

• Keswick
 • Rakefoot
 ▲ WALLA CRAG
BLEABERRY
 ▲ FELL
• Lodore

MILES
0   1   2   3

from near Rakefoot

NATURAL FEATURES

The pleasant Vale of Keswick, surely one of earth's sweetest landscapes, is surrounded by mountains of noble proportions with an inner circle of lesser fells which deserve more than the name of foothills, each having strong individual characteristics, a definite and distinctive appearance, and a natural beauty all its own. Among these is Walla Crag, an eminence of intermingled rocks and trees overlooking the east shore of lovely Derwent Water: of moderate elevation yet steep, romantic, challenging. Seen from the lake the hoary top seems unattainable, yet it may be gained by the gentlest of ascents for the slopes beyond the upper fringe of crag descend easily, accompanied by Brockle Beck, almost to the streets of Keswick.

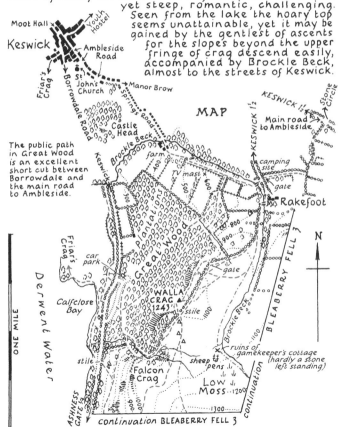

The public path in Great Wood is an excellent short cut between Borrowdale and the main road to Ambleside.

205

ASCENT FROM KESWICK
1000 feet of ascent : 2½ miles

On a first visit it is easy to go astray here. The good cart-track from Rakefoot continues (soon deteriorating) in the direction of Bleaberry Fell: the less distinct branch path to Walla Crag follows the wall round to the right. Parties have been found toiling up Bleaberry Fell under the impression that they were climbing Walla Crag, an excusable mistake, for the former comes clearly into view ahead from the cart-track while the latter is out of sight, and, in any case, is not conspicuous from this side. A signpost would be useful at this point.

Note that an exciting (but unofficial) path passes through the kissing gate, and skirts the edge of the escarpment on its way to the summit, providing excellent views en route.

The iron grid in the cart-track was installed by the Army to facilitate the passage of tanks during the war, when the fell was a training ground.

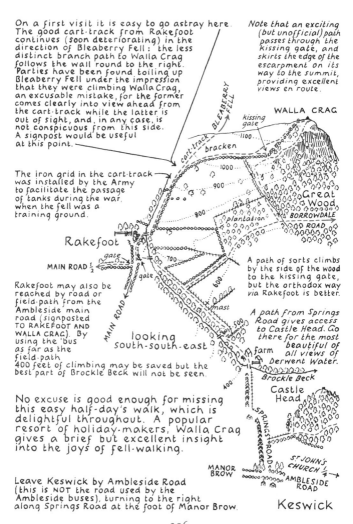

A path of sorts climbs by the side of the wood to the kissing gate, but the orthodox way via Rakefoot is better.

Rakefoot may also be reached by road or field-path from the Ambleside main road (signposted TO RAKEFOOT AND WALLA CRAG). By using the 'bus as far as the field-path 400 feet of climbing may be saved but the best part of Brockle Beck will not be seen.

A path from Springs Road gives access to Castle Head. Go there for the most beautiful of all views of Derwent Water.

No excuse is good enough for missing this easy half-day's walk, which is delightful throughout. A popular resort of holiday-makers, Walla Crag gives a brief but excellent insight into the joys of fell-walking.

Leave Keswick by Ambleside Road (this is NOT the road used by the Ambleside buses), turning to the right along Springs Road at the foot of Manor Brow.

looking south-south-east

ASCENT FROM THE BORROWDALE ROAD
950 feet of ascent : 1 mile (2½ from Keswick)

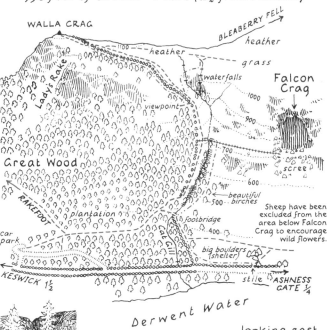

looking east

Alternative starts are given. The 'purest' route is that from the car park, which keeps throughout to the Walla Crag side of Cat Gill, but trees shut out views that are too good to be missed. This defect may be remedied by starting from the stile 150 yards beyond the point where the road crosses Cat Gill. At 400' cross the gill by way of a footbridge, avoiding the necessity for a difficult crossing at 700'. The path up the south bank of Cat Gill is going out of use, making it harder to visit the base of Falcon Crag.

A beautiful short climb up steep colourful slopes overlooking Derwent Water. If the starting point on the road is reached via Friar's Crag and Calfclose Bay, and if the return is made via Rakefoot and Brockle Beck, this becomes the best walk easily attainable in a half-day from Keswick.

Waterfalls in Cat Gill

THE SUMMIT

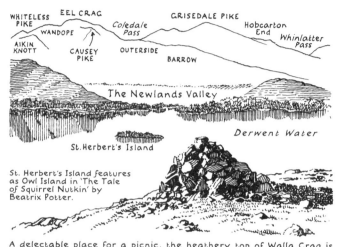

WHITELESS PIKE — EEL CRAG — Coledale Pass — GRISEDALE PIKE — Hobcarton End — Whinlatter Pass — WANDOPE — AIKIN KNOTT — CAUSEY PIKE — OUTERSIDE — BARROW

The Newlands Valley

Derwent Water

St. Herbert's Island

St. Herbert's Island features as Owl Island in 'The Tale of Squirrel Nutkin' by Beatrix Potter.

A delectable place for a picnic, the heathery top of Walla Crag is also a favourite viewpoint for Derwent Water, seen directly below the long steep escarpment. A profusion of decayed tree stumps indicates that the summit, now bare, was at one time thickly wooded. The summit-cairn must have moved since it was illustrated; it now stands well away from the precipice.

DESCENTS: Keep to the paths: the dangers of straying from them should be obvious. An inviting opening in the cliff (Lady's Rake) 150 yards south of the cairn, is a trap to be avoided. *In mist*, note that the wall links Rakefoot and the Borrowdale road, and that the paths follow it. The descent to Rakefoot is easy; the other route (recently improved) is steep.

WALLA CRAG — RAKEFOOT — 1100

ASHNESS BRIDGE — 1100 — heather 1200 — 1300 — 1400 — × sheepfold — 1500 — 1600 — 1700 — 1800 — 1900 — heather — BLEABERRY FELL

N

HALF A MILE

RIDGE ROUTE

TO BLEABERRY FELL, 1932'
1¼ miles : S, then SSE curving SE
Depression at 1070'
900 feet of ascent
A dull climb relieved by fine views

Start along the Ashness Bridge path, turning left at a cairn. Above the sheepfold the path is a ribbon of gravel and easy to follow. The steepest part of the route is paved with rocks.

208

THE VIEW

This well-known view has earned its popularity not by its extensiveness but by the variety and charm of many nearby features, with Borrowdale an outstanding study of mountain grouping and the exciting downward prospect of Derwent Water of more general appeal. An interesting emphasis is placed on the relatively low elevation of much of the central part of Lakeland by the distant view of Grey Friar in the Coniston fells — hardly to be expected from Walla Crag's modest height so far to the north.

Principal Fells

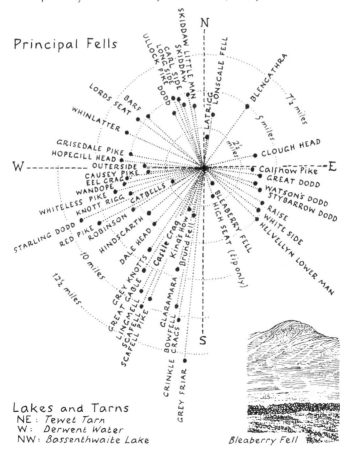

Bleaberry Fell

Lakes and Tarns
NE : Tewet Tarn
W : Derwent Water
NW : Bassenthwaite Lake

17 Heughscar Hill
from Askham

Heughscar Hill is one of the Lake District's minor fells, recorded by Wainwright in his 'mopping-up' operation in *The Outlying Fells of Lakeland*. But as he frequently pointed out, fells like this often have at least as much to offer as many grander peaks from his seven *Pictorial Guides*, and they tend to be well suited to young walkers in particular. 'Heughscar Hill is a gem for aged fellwalkers,' says Wainwright in his notes – and so it is for families, too.

Starting from the peaceful village of Askham – 'Westmorland's most attractive', in Wainwright's opinion – the route soon reaches the target of Heughscar Hill, a flat, grassy and open space that is ideal for energetic children and with fine views down towards Ullswater and surrounding fells. But this is only one of the highlights of this outstanding walk, which follows sections of High Street, the old Roman road that once linked forts at Penrith and Ambleside and that gives its name to a fell to the south. As Wainwright notes, the occupying Romans would have known Heughscar Hill well, and walkers today will be following in their footsteps for stretches.

The route also takes in several stone circles, of which there are many in this part of the Lake District – proof that the region was well trodden even before the Romans made their mark. They include a circle known as the Cockpit by one of the junctions with High Street, and the Cop Stone, a metre-wide leaning monolith that probably formed part of a Bronze Age ring cairn on Moor Divock. With smaller circles, piles of stones and more recent boundary markers to spot as well, it makes for a great open-air history lesson as you walk.

Heughscar Hill is one of the longest walks in this book, but the walking throughout is very easy, over good paths and with gentle inclines and long sections that are entirely flat. To shorten the walk by about ¾ mile, continue driving through

Askham as indicated by the directions, park just after the cattle-grid and pick up the route at point 2. If children are flagging towards the end, another 1 mile or so can be saved by omitting the detour to the Cop Stone.

From *The Outlying Fells of Lakeland*

Distance 7 miles (11.3km)

Ascent 750 feet (230m)

Start and finish point The car park by Askham's Village Hall and swimming pool adjacent to the Queen's Head pub (NY 513 237)

Ordnance Survey maps Explorer OL5; Landranger 90

Getting there

Askham is about five miles south of Penrith. Follow the A6 out of town, but soon turn right to take the B5320 towards Pooley Bridge and Ullswater. Soon after passing through the village of Yanwath, turn left to Askham. Look for the signposts for parking, the village hall and swimming pool, on the left from this direction. Parking is free, but donations in a box are invited for the upkeep of the hall and swimming pool.

If you are driving from the south, make for Shap, just off junction 39 of the M6. Quiet minor roads take you from here to Askham via Bampton and Helton, but the quicker way is north along the A6, turning left at Hackthorpe.

Askham is served direct only by the 111 bus from Penrith, which runs only twice on Tuesdays, giving you enough time to complete the walk in between. The 106 between Penrith and Kendal is much more frequent, running from early to late from Mondays to Saturdays, and stops at the entrance to the Lowther Estate, a short walk from Askham.

Facilities, food and drink

Askham is a delightful village with pretty greens and attractive whitewashed cottages. It has a couple of good children and dog-friendly pubs – the Queen's Head, right by the start of the walk (01931 712225, www.queensheadaskham. com), and the Punchbowl Inn, on the road west towards the Lowther Estate (01931 712443, www.punchbowlaskham. com). The village shop, Askham Stores, is also close to the start of the walk (01931 712187).

It is a surprise to most visitors to find that the village boasts its own swimming pools, including one for small children. They are open-air but thankfully, given the Cumbrian climate, heated. A kiosk sells food and it is a great place for families on a nice day. It opens in the summer months; check in advance for times (01931 712292, www.askhamandhelton. co.uk).

The nearby Lowther Estate has plenty more for families to see and do, including a splendid castle, recently restored after years of crumbling, and extensive grounds with woodland, a deer park and lots of footpaths to follow (01931 712192, www. lowthercastle.org). The walled garden of the Lowther estate hosts the Lakeland Bird of Prey Centre, where children can see a variety of birds and watch flying demonstrations (01931 712746). The estate hosts frequent events including an annual country fair in August, and has holiday cottages for hire.

Directions

1 Return to the road from the car park and turn left, immediately passing the Queen's Head pub. Turn right at the junction by the pub. (Askham Stores is a few steps further on if you want to pick up supplies first.) This quiet road soon forks; take the right-hand branch and rise up past houses. It reaches a cattle-grid, with parking spaces just beyond.

2 At the end of the parking spaces, branch off from the road to the right to pick up a broad track with a wall on the right.

After about ½ mile, the track passes a stone barn on your right and thins out. Where it forks, just beyond, ignore the path curving left to take a fainter path over grass up to a wooden gate (NY 498 230). Go through and follow the path beyond, with trees soon on your right. Over the brow of the first rise the path becomes fainter, but aim for the left-hand edge of the strip of plantation ahead. Reach this after ½ mile from the gate, and follow the ruined wall enclosing the plantation up to its top corner. Continue in the same direction ahead. The grassy path to the top now forks twice; bear right at the first junction and left at the second to reach the small rough cairn on the summit of Heughscar Hill (NY 488 232).

3 Continue in the same direction on a grassy path, with Ullswater down to your left and outcrops of rock on the right, to cross Heugh Scar. Drop down beyond to a clear, firm path, and turn left along it. Ignore all side-tracks to continue in the same direction for ¾ mile, the second half of this stretch over grass rather than stone, to a cairn at a junction of paths (NY 483 227). Continue over the junction and walk on for 500m to an ancient circle of stones called the Cockpit. Turn left here and walk for just over 500m more to another junction. (A few steps to the left here is an old boundary stone.) Turn right at this junction, and follow the clear path for a little under 1 mile to the Cop Stone (NY 496 216).

4 Retrace your steps from here, and after just over 200m look for a path to the right. It is the second of two in short succession; the correct one immediately rises over a series of small humps and, another 200m on, passes another ancient stone circle. The path beyond this gets fainter, but aim at first for the left-hand edge of the middle of three strips of trees ahead. This leads on to a more distinct path, which traverses the hillside to return you to the right of the same strip of trees, where you will find the gate crossed earlier. Return down the track to the next gate and then down the road to Askham.

Heughscar Hill
1231'
750 feet of ascent

from the
Stone Circle

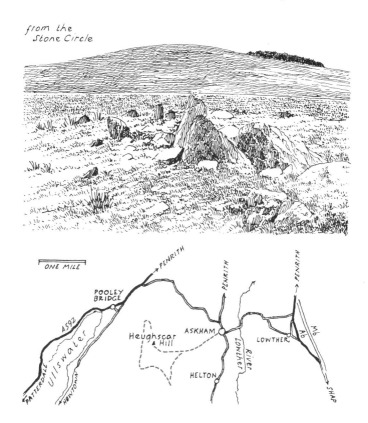

ONE MILE

PENRITH

POOLEY BRIDGE

A592

PATTERDALE

ULLSWATER

HOWTOWN

Heughscar Hill

ASKHAM

HELTON

PENRITH

LOWTHER

River Lowther

PENRITH

A6

SHAP

M6

214

The Romans knew Heughscar Hill, though not by that name, and laid their High Street along its western flank. Today, pony-trekkers enjoy this historic highway.

Heughscar Hill is the gentlest of eminences. It is easily reached by a stroll from Westmorland's most attractive village, Askham, and commands a fine prospect, including a lovely view of Ullswater with the lofty Helvellyn range forming a majestic background. It is clothed in patches of bracken and a velvet turf on which carpet slippers would be more appropriate than boots, but its greatest joy is the spine of limestone outcropping in rocky pavements along the top.

The hill overlooks a rough plateau, Moor Divock, the site of many antiquities, suggesting that long before the Romans came the ancient Britons had already found the place to their liking.

So will modern Britons, especially those hovering on the verge of becoming ancient. Heughscar Hill is a gem for aged fellwalkers.

Ullswater, from the summit

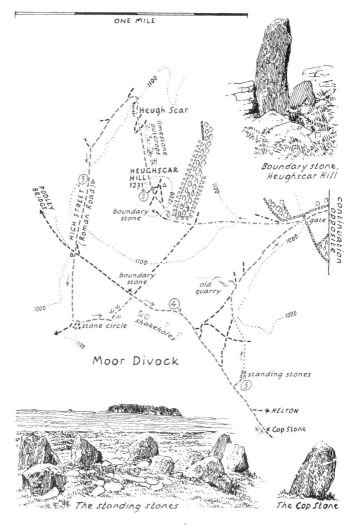

ONE MILE

Heugh Scar

limestone outcrops

HEUGHSCAR HILL 1231

boundary stone

POOLEY BRIDGE

HIGH STREET (Roman Road)

③

②

1100

1100

1000

gate

continuation opposite

Boundary stone, Heughscar Hill

boundary stone

old quarry

1100

stone circle

shakeholes

④

1000

Moor Divock

standing stones

⑤

HELTON

Cop Stone

1100

The standing stones

The Cop Stone

216

MAP

Depart from Askham, a charming village,
by the rising street to the west, which ends
at a cattle grid. A good path goes ahead with
a wall on the right. Ignore a tarmac strip and
later a gravel road both branching left, keeping
uphill, now on grass, to a gate giving access to open fell.
Indefinite tracks lead forward: take the one up a gentle
incline, on lovely turf, aiming for the corner of a plantation
half a mile ahead. Go along the side of the plantation and
then bear right and left to the cairn indicating the top of
Heughscar Hill, where a lovely view of Ullswater is seen
backed by Helvellyn; to the east the Cross Fell range stands
up well. Green turf and natural rock gardens of limestone
make this a delectable place on a sunny day.

Continue north along the top, with a line of outcropping
rock on the right, and over the limestone crag (Heugh Scar),
seen in profile ahead, descending beyond it in bracken to
join a clear path running below it. Follow this to the left.
Diversions created by pony-trekkers have in places obscured
the original course of the path (the Roman High Street): a
line taken west of south will, however, reach a wide green
track (Pooley Bridge to Helton) at a cairn. Go across this,
continuing south on the High Street, to a stone circle (called
the Cockpit, according to the Ordnance Survey map), from
which cut across to the green track and follow it southeast
as far as the Cop Stone, prominently seen on the skyline. Now
retrace steps for a quarter-mile and then turn onto the moor
on the right to find, in 100 yards, a tidy cluster of standing
stones (described as a cairn circle on the Ordnance Survey
map). All these relics are of great age. Being an antiquity
yourself, it boosts morale exceedingly to find things even
older than you are. With an inspired new buoyancy of stride
(but, please, no singing) scamper across the moor north to
join a path leading to the scanty remains of a quarry, where
a simple traverse northeast leads back to the fell gate.

Return thence to Askham by the outward route.

217

18 Haystacks
from Gatesgarth

No book of walks connected with Wainwright is complete without Haystacks, for this was one of his very favourite fells. 'For beauty, variety and interesting detail, for sheer fascination and unique individuality, the summit-area of Haystacks is supreme,' he wrote in his notes. 'This is in fact the best fell-top of all – a place of great charm and fairyland attractiveness.'

It is also the place where Wainwright's ashes were scattered after his death in 1991. 'All I ask for, at the end, is a last long resting place by the side of Innominate Tarn, on Haystacks, where the water gently laps the gravelly shore and the heather blooms and Pillar and Gable keep unfailing watch,' he wrote in his memoirs. 'A quiet place, a lonely place. I shall go to it, for the last time, and be carried: someone who knew me in life will take me and empty me out of a little box and leave me there alone. And if you, dear reader, should get a bit of grit in your boot as you are crossing Haystacks in the year to come, please treat it with respect. It might be me.'

Not least because of Wainwright's endorsement, Haystacks has become a very popular climb, and its paths are now well worn. This walk combines the two routes described by Wainwright from Gatesgarth into a fine round, climbing via the crossroads of walkers' paths at Scarth Gap and descending alongside two mountain streams, Black Beck and Warnscale Beck. In between it traverses the top of the fell, one of the most peaceful of all Lake District summits and a great place for children to linger for an hour or two and investigate. As well as scores of rocky outcrops, it is home to two sizeable and beautiful tarns – Wainwright's requested resting place of Innominate Tarn, where a discreet plaque marks the fact; and Blackbeck Tarn, the larger of the two and, because it is a few steps off the path, usually quieter and the better place to rest. The views, which include many of the highest fells in the Lakes, are terrific too.

Although the paths are generally well defined throughout, this can be a challenging climb for small children. The final pull to the top is over rocks that require a bit of scrambling, while the descent via Warnscale is down paths that are steep and loose in places; follow the alternative descent suggested in the directions if children will find this too difficult. But despite these challenges and the fair amount of climbing involved, walkers of all ages now flock to Haystacks, and for good reason. For a day's excursion in the north Lakes, and as a tribute to Wainwright, it is hard to beat.

From *Book Seven: The Western Fells*

Distance 4½ miles (7.2km)

Ascent 1,550 feet (470m)

Start and finish point The car park at Gatesgarth Farm (NY 195 150)

Ordnance Survey maps Explorer OL4; Landranger 89 or 90

Getting there
Gatesgarth is at the south end of Buttermere lake, about two miles from Buttermere village on the B5289. It can be reached from Keswick by following the B5289 through Borrowdale and over the Honister Pass; or by heading west a short distance to Braithwaite and then following the road through the Newlands valley to Buttermere. The car park by Gatesgarth Farm is pay-and-display. If it is full there are some free roadside spaces further up the Honister Pass on the B5289 in the Borrowdale direction.

The only bus to serve Gatesgarth is the number 77, a popular service for walkers that runs daily from early April to early November. It runs four times a day in both directions on a circular route from Keswick that takes in Portinscale, Grange, the Honister Slate Mine, Buttermere, Lorton and Whinlatter. Gatesgarth is about halfway round the circuit, so it doesn't matter which direction you follow from Keswick.

Facilities, food and drink

Gatesgarth has no shops or pubs, though there is sometimes a van by the farm selling ice creams and refreshments. The nearest facilities are two miles away in Buttermere, which has pubs including the Bridge Hotel (017687 770252, www.bridge-hotel.com) and cafés including the Syke Farm tea rooms (017687 70222). You can pay your respects to Wainwright in Buttermere in the tiny St James's church, which has a plaque dedicated to him beneath a window that frames this fell, with the instruction: 'Lift your eyes to Haystacks, his favourite place.'

Three miles along the B5289 in the other direction is the Honister Slate Mine, which has a café as well as an interesting visitor centre, tours of the underground mine and a via ferrata high-wire adventure trail (017687 77230, www.honister.com). The centre is a good introduction to the mining that has shaped the Lake District fells over the centuries.

Directions

1 Cross the road from the car park and pick up the footpath signed for Buttermere. It cuts across the farmyard and then continues beyond on a broad farm track, with Buttermere lake over to your right, up to an old bridge – called Peggy's Bridge – and a wooden gate. Climb beyond this, the way signposted for Scarth Gap, to pass to the right of a triangle of trees. At the far corner of the triangle, the path bends to the left to follow its top edge, then leaves the trees to climb, now with the lake to your back and stone steps under your feet. The crinkled top of Haystacks lies ahead to the left. The path is very clear as it rises up and, just under 1 mile from

the car park, reaches a flat area with large stones that makes a good resting point.

2 About ¼ mile on from here, and with a gap in a broken dry stone wall halfway between, the path reaches Scarth Gap. After crossing this flat area, beyond a large cairn and just before some old metal gateposts (NY 189 133), the path forks off to the left; follow this. The way now zig-zags up the slope, with the direction to the top clear, although short cuts have created additional paths in places; if in any doubt, look for the cairns to guide you up. Some light scrambling is required to reach the summit area, which is marked by a host of cairns on different tops (NY 194 132). See Wainwright's notes and sketch plan of the top if you want to reach the true summit.

3 Continue on in the same direction towards the tarn, Innominate Tarn, that lies ahead. The path follows the tarn along its left-hand edge, and then drops a little to cross a fell stream – Black Beck. Turn to the right here for a few steps up to the corner of Blackbeck Tarn (NY 201 129). Back on the path, continue ahead in your original direction until, as you pull level with an impressive crag away to your right, Little Round How, the path splits (NY 206 132). Take the left-hand fork to descend. (For a slightly gentler descent in return for about ½ mile more walking, take the right-hand path here and turn left when it meets the old Dubs Quarry road, a smoother track on the other side of the beck.)

4 The path is rough in places at first, and care is needed with small children. Ignore the temptations to cross the beck to the path on the other side, and keep on the left of it throughout the descent. Just over ¾ mile from the fork, the path reaches the valley floor by a footbridge (NY 199 137). Cross this and take the easy path beyond, through bracken. Just over ¾ mile further on, it reaches the road at Gatesgarth. Turn left for the car park.

Haystacks

properly
Hay Stacks
(two words)
as on
Ordnance maps

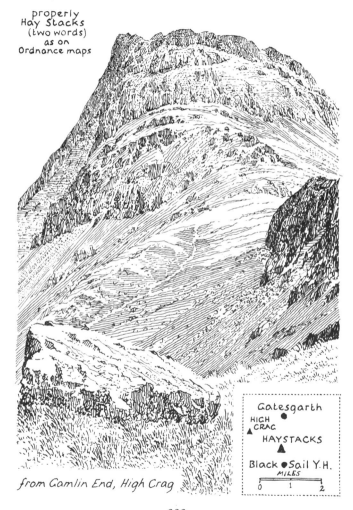

Gatesgarth
HIGH •
▲ CRAG
HAYSTACKS
▲
Black • Sail Y.H.
MILES
0   1   2

from Gamlin End, High Crag

NATURAL FEATURES

Haystacks stands unabashed and unashamed in the midst of a circle of much loftier fells, like a shaggy terrier in the company of foxhounds, some of them known internationally, but not one of this distinguished group of mountains around Ennerdale and Buttermere can show a greater variety and a more fascinating arrangement of interesting features. Here are sharp peaks in profusion, tarns with islands and tarns without islands, crags, screes, rocks for climbing and rocks not for climbing, heather tracts, marshes, serpentine trails, tarns with streams and tarns with no streams. All these, with a background of magnificent landscapes, await every visitor to Haystacks but they will be appreciated most by those who go there to linger and explore. It is a place of surprises around corners, and there are many corners. For a man trying to get a persistent worry out of his mind, the top of Haystacks is a wonderful cure.

The fell rises between the deep hollow of Warnscale Bottom near Gatesgarth, and Ennerdale: between a valley familiar to summer motorists and a valley reached only on foot. It is bounded on the west by Scarth Gap, a pass linking the two. The Buttermere aspect is the better known, although this side is often dark in shadow and seen only as a silhouette against the sky: here, above Warnscale, is a great wall of crags. The Ennerdale flank, open to the sun, is friendlier but steep and rough nevertheless.

Eastwards, beyond the tangle of tors and outcrops forming the boundary of Haystacks on this side, a broad grass slope rises easily and unattractively to Brandreth on the edge of the Borrowdale watershed; beyond is Derwent country.

The spelling of Haystacks as one word is a personal preference of the author (and others), and probably arises from a belief that the name originated from the resemblance of the scattered tors on the summit to stacks of hay in a field. If this were so, the one word *Haystacks* would be correct (as it is in *Haycock*). But learned authorities state that the name derives from the Icelandic 'stack', meaning 'a columnar rock', and that the true interpretation is *High Rocks*. This is logical and appropriate. *High Rocks* is a name of two words and would be wrongly written as *Highrocks*.

The summit tarn

Big Stack,
looking east from a point
near the path to the
summit from
Scarth Gap.

In the picture below
Big Stack appears on
the extreme right.

The north crags,
looking west from the
slopes of Green Crag.

The path is seen
skirting the cliff
on the left.

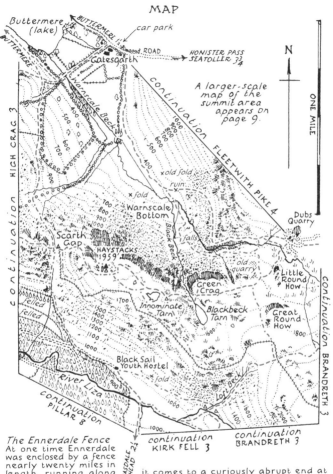

MAP

A larger-scale map of the summit area appears on page 9.

The Ennerdale Fence

At one time Ennerdale was enclosed by a fence nearly twenty miles in length, running along both watersheds and around the head of the valley. The fence was mainly of post and wire, and in most places only the posts survive. On Haystacks the fence has been restored, but it comes to a curiously abrupt end at Scarth Gap. In general, the line of the fence followed parish boundaries but on Haystacks there is considerable deviation. Here the series of iron stakes embedded in rock (erected to mark the boundary of the Lonsdale estate) coincides with the parish boundary, but the fence keeps well to the south of this line.

ASCENT FROM GATESGARTH
1550 feet of ascent : 1¼ miles

via SCARTH GAP

From Scarth Gap a well-constructed path leads up to the summit, avoiding all scree, though in places it is necessary to handle rock.

HAYSTACKS

Big Stack

Stack Rake

Scarth Gap

HIGH CRAG

High Wax Knott

Low Wax Knott

It is a test of iron discipline to pass without halting several large *comfortable* boulders athwart the path.

Scarth Gap is one of the pleasantest of the foot-passes. Apart from the steep section above the old sheepfold, the gradients are gentle and the views both ahead and behind are full of interest. The path is generally good, and the roughness formerly encountered on the early stages of the climb is buried underneath a new conifer plantation.

Coupled with a return by the Warnscale route to make a full 'round' journey, the ascent of Haystacks via the pass of Scarth Gap is a prelude of much merit and beauty to a mountain walk of unique character, the whole distance being no more than five miles. Save it, however, for a fine clear day.

Leave Gatesgarth by the bridge, at a signpost to Ennerdale.

gate

bracken

old sheepfold

Gatesgarth

ROAD

car park

Buttermere

BUTTERMERE via BURTNESS WOOD

looking south

ASCENT FROM GATESGARTH
via WARNSCALE

1600 feet of ascent : 2¼ miles

HAYSTACKS

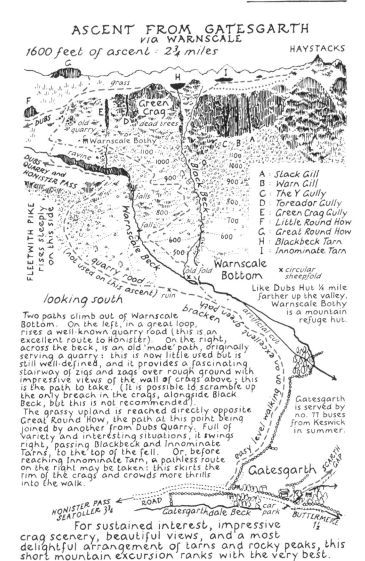

looking south

A : Slack Gill
B : Warn Gill
C : The Y Gully
D : Toreador Gully
E : Green Crag Gully
F : Little Round How
G : Great Round How
H : Blackbeck Tarn
I : Innominate Tarn

x *circular sheepfold*

Like Dubs Hut ¼ mile farther up the valley, Warnscale Bothy is a mountain refuge hut.

Gatesgarth is served by no. 77 buses from Keswick in summer.

Two paths climb out of Warnscale Bottom. On the left, in a great loop, rises a well-known quarry road (this is an excellent route to Honister). On the right, across the beck, is an old 'made' path, originally serving a quarry: this is now little used but is still well-defined, and it provides a fascinating stairway of zigs and zags over rough ground with impressive views of the wall of crags above; this is the path to take. (It is possible to scramble up the only breach in the crags, alongside Black Beck, but this is not recommended.)
The grassy upland is reached directly opposite Great Round How, the path at this point being joined by another from Dubs Quarry. Full of variety and interesting situations, it swings right, passing Blackbeck and Innominate Tarns, to the top of the fell. Or, before reaching Innominate Tarn, a pathless route on the right may be taken: this skirts the rim of the crags and crowds more thrills into the walk.

For sustained interest, impressive crag scenery, beautiful views, and a most delightful arrangement of tarns and rocky peaks, this short mountain excursion ranks with the very best.

ASCENT FROM HONISTER PASS
1050 feet of ascent : 2¾ miles

A note of explanation is required. This ascent-route does not conform to the usual pattern, being more in the nature of an upland cross-country walk than a mountain climb : there are two pronounced descents before foot is set on Haystacks. The wide variety of scene and the fascinating intricacies of the path are justification for the inclusion of the route in this book.

HAYSTACKS

If returning to Honister, note the path to Brandreth just below Innominate Tarn. It is marked by a cairn, but it is very difficult to follow. By using this until it joins the Great Gable path and then swinging left around Dubs Bottom, the Drum House can be regained without extra effort or time.

After traversing the back of Green Crag the path drops to the outlet of Blackbeck Tarn, rising stonily therefrom with a profound abyss on the right. This section is the highlight of the walk.

looking west

From the hut at Dubs Quarry leave the road and go down to the stream, crossing it (by stepping stones) where its silent meanderings through the Dubs marshes assume a noisy urgency.

From the top of Honister Pass Haystacks is nowhere in sight, and even when it comes into view, after crossing the shoulder of Fleetwith Pike at the Drum House, it is insignificant against the towering background of Pillar, being little higher in altitude and seemingly remote across the wide depression of Dubs Bottom. But, although the route here described is not a natural approach, the elevation of Honister Pass, its car-parking facilities, and the unerring pointer of the tramway make access to Haystacks particularly convenient from this point.

228

ASCENT FROM ENNERDALE
(BLACK SAIL YOUTH HOSTEL)

970 feet of ascent
1¼ miles

looking north

This route is likely to be of interest only to those staying at the magnificently situated Black Sail Youth Hostel. This hostel is open to everyone, but those intending to use it are advised to book well in advance.

formerly a shepherd's hut,.....

Black Sail Youth Hostel

THE SUMMIT

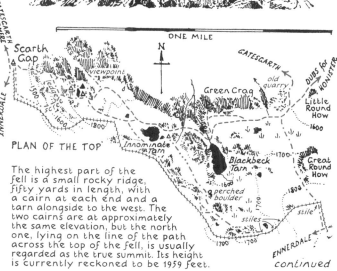

PLAN OF THE TOP

The highest part of the
fell is a small rocky ridge,
fifty yards in length, with
a cairn at each end and a
tarn alongside to the west. The
two cairns are at approximately
the same elevation, but the north
one, lying on the line of the path
across the top of the fell, is usually
regarded as the true summit. Its height
is currently reckoned to be 1959 feet.

continued

230

THE SUMMIT

continued

Haystacks fails to qualify for inclusion in the author's "best half-dozen" only because of inferior height, a deficiency in vertical measurement. Another thousand feet would have made all the difference.

But for beauty, variety and interesting detail, for sheer fascination and unique individuality, the summit-area of Haystacks is supreme. This is in fact the best fell-top of all — a place of great charm and fairyland attractiveness. Seen from a distance, these qualities are not suspected: indeed, on the contrary, the appearance of Haystacks is almost repellent when viewed from the higher surrounding peaks: black are its bones and black is its flesh. With its thick covering of heather it is dark and sombre even when the sun sparkles the waters of its many tarns, gloomy and mysterious even under a blue sky. There are fierce crags and rough screes and outcrops that will be grittier still when the author's ashes are scattered here.✕

Yet the combination of features, of tarn and tor, of cliff and cove, the labyrinth of corners and recesses, the maze of old sheepwalks and paths, form a design, or a lack of design, of singular appeal and absorbing interest. One can forget even a raging toothache on Haystacks.

✕ *After his death in 1991,*
Wainwright's ashes were
duly scattered
on Haystacks.

perched boulder
on a rock platform

Note the profile
in shadow.
Some women
have faces
like that.

On a first visit, learn thoroughly the details of the mile-long main path across the top, a magnificent traverse, because this serves as the best introduction to the geography of the fell.

Having memorised this, several interesting deviations may be made: the parallel alternative above the rim of the north face, the scramble onto Big Stack, the 'cross-country' route around the basin of Blackbeck Tarn, the walk alongside the fence, and so on.

typical summit tors

DESCENTS : A well-made path starts just west of the summit and leads down to Scarth Gap. An alternative path farther south is marred by loose stones and should be avoided. It is advisable to regard the whole of the north edge as highly dangerous. The only advice that can be given to a novice lost on Haystacks *in mist* is that he should kneel down and pray for safe deliverance.

THE VIEW

This is not a case of distance lending enchantment to the view, because apart from a glimpse of Skiddaw above the Robinson-Hindscarth depression and a slice of the Helvellyn range over Honister, the scene is predominantly one of high mountains within a five-mile radius. And really good they look — the enchantment is close at hand. Set in a tight surround, they are seen in revealing detail: a rewarding study deserving leisurely appreciation.

Principal Fells

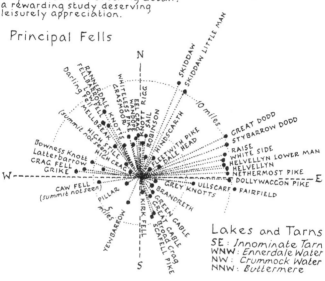

Lakes and Tarns
SE : Innominate Tarn
WNW : Ennerdale Water
NW : Crummock Water
NNW : Buttermere

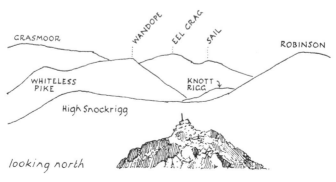

looking north

RIDGE ROUTES

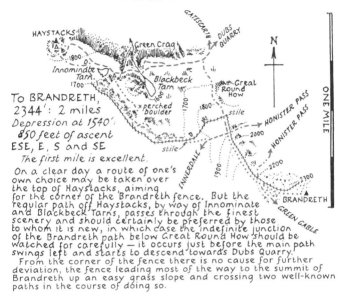

HAYSTACKS
Green Crag
GATESGARTH
DUBS QUARRY
Innominate Tarn
1800
1700
Blackbeck Tarn
× perched boulder
1800
Great Round How
stile
N
ONE MILE
1700
1800
stile
ENNERDALE
1900
HONISTER PASS
HONISTER PASS
2000
2200
2300
BRANDRETH
GREEN GABLE

TO BRANDRETH, 2344': 2 miles
Depression at 1540':
850 feet of ascent
ESE, E, S and SE

The first mile is excellent.

On a clear day a route of one's own choice may be taken over the top of Haystacks, aiming for the corner of the Brandreth fence. But the regular path off Haystacks, by way of Innominate and Blackbeck Tarns, passes through the finest scenery and should certainly be preferred by those to whom it is new, in which case the indefinite junction of the Brandreth path below Great Round How should be watched for carefully — it occurs just before the main path swings left and starts to descend towards Dubs Quarry.

From the corner of the fence there is no cause for further deviation, the fence leading most of the way to the summit of Brandreth up an easy grass slope and crossing two well-known paths in the course of doing so.

TO HIGH CRAG, 2443'
1¼ miles : W, then NW
Depression at 1425' (Scarth Gap)
1100 feet of ascent
A fine walk in spite of scree

Follow faithfully the well-made path to the west from the summit, a delightful game of ins and outs and ups and downs. An alternative path south of the summit encounters an area of loose stones and should be avoided. From Scarth Gap a beautiful path climbs through the heather to Seat; then a good ridge follows to the final tower of High Crag: this deteriorates badly into slippery scree on the later stages of the ascent.

HIGH CRAG
2300
2100
2000
1900
1800
BUTTERMERE
tarn
Seat
N
1700
1600
Scarth Gap
1500
HAYSTACKS

High Crag, from Scarth Gap

HALF A MILE

19 Maiden Moor
from Grange

With 1,600 feet of height to be attained, Maiden Moor is one of the sterner challenges in this book. But the climbing is a steady slog rather than a steep scramble, and more confident young walkers will find it a good test of their abilities.

It also makes a nice introduction to longer and more taxing Lake District horseshoe walks, sitting as it does in the middle of a popular ridge route that takes in Catbells (covered in Chapter 14 of this book), High Spy, Dale Head and more. Those who want to extend their day will find it easy enough to add one or more of these peaks to the walk, which follows Wainwright's suggested ascent from Grange via Manesty – 'a beautiful climb, very suitable for those who prefer to have an unloseable path under their feet', as he called it. In fact, the fell's biggest tests may well be on top of the exposed moor, where walkers can get buffeted by winds; or coming down on the route via Nitting Haws and Swanesty How, which is steep in places and needs some care to be sure of the route. These challenges, plus the height, make it a substantial excursion, but one that will be within the abilities of most families with a little walking experience over the course of a day.

As Wainwright points out in his notes, the views from the highest points of Maiden Moor are limited – 'the scene is satisfactory' is about the best he can manage to say for it – but the panoramas on the approach before and after Hause Gate are much better, so don't forget to turn round while puffing your way up. Other interesting features of Maiden Moor include its role in several of Beatrix Potter's books, and its attractive name, the source of which is not known for sure, though it may refer to a place where maidens gathered or played.

From *Book Six: The North Western Fells*

Distance 4½ miles (7.2km)

Ascent 1,600 feet (490m)

Start and finish point The car park by the Methodist Church in Grange (NY 254 175)

Ordnance Survey maps Explorer OL4; Landranger 89 or 90

Getting there

The car park by the Methodist Church is reached immediately after crossing the bridge over the River Derwent into Grange from the B5289, the road into the Borrowdale valley about 4 miles south of Keswick. Make a donation in the Church's boxes in return for parking. There are only a few spaces, so try to get there early if the weather is fine. More parking is available by the roadside further up through Grange on the first stretch of the walk, including by the village's other church, but take good care not to obstruct traffic. Proper car parks are available back on the B5289; the largest is the National Trust one for the Bowder Stone, signposted soon after the Grange turn on the left in the Borrowdale direction.

This is a good walk to start and finish by bus from Keswick. Take the 77 service in the clockwise direction, and ask for the Manesty stop, which will save you the first ¾ mile of walking from Grange; and return on the anti-clockwise service after refreshments in the village. There are four services a day in each direction between early April and early November, so plan your schedule carefully, though there is ample time to fit in this walk. Grange Bridge can also be reached all year round on the open-top 78 bus from Keswick to Borrowdale.

Facilities, food and drink

Walkers are well catered for in Grange, with two pleasant cafés: the Grange Bridge Cottage Tearooms near the river (017687

77201); and the Grange Café, a short stroll further into the village (017687 77077). Keswick has the closest shops, and the nearest pub is the Scafell Hotel further down the Borrowdale valley at Rosthwaite (017687 77208, www.scafell.co.uk).

The river by the car park in Grange is a good spot to refresh tired feet, and children will enjoy the shallow water and stone skimming. Before returning to the car, it is worth visiting the Methodist Church to see its exhibition about the local area called The Borrowdale Story (www.theborrowdalestory. co.uk). Other interesting stopping points include the Bowder Stone, a short drive south from Grange Bridge; and the Lodore Falls, waterfalls that are spectacular after rain and that can be accessed near the hotel of the same name on the road back to Keswick.

Directions

1 Leave the car park to walk away from the bridge on the road through the village and past its two tearooms. After ¾ mile, just after a cluster of houses at Manesty, leave the road to the half left on a stony path, the way indicated by a public footpath sign (NY 251 185). This starts to rise, very soon passing a large wooden gate and continuing steadily upwards on a broad path. After about 250m the path forks; take the left-hand option to continue rising, with glorious views of Derwent Water opening up on the right. After ¼ mile more, the way reaches Hause Gate, a junction of paths on a flat area (NY 244 192).

2 (From Hause Gate Cat Bells is over to the right, and it can be added to the walk with a short there-and-back round.) Bear left to begin the pull up towards the broad expanse of Maiden Moor, quite sharply at first but soon easing out with more terrific views over the valley. The path is very clear as it leads for about ¾ mile up to the area around Bull Crag (NY 237 182) that is normally taken to be the highest point, though no-one is quite sure of the exact spot.

3 Another ¾ mile of walking on the clear path leads across the area known as Narrow Moor until a large pile of stones is reached. Turn left here towards the cairn perched on rocks about 100m away (NY 237 171). Continue on in the same direction, but 150m further bear left just in front of some low crags to pass them close by on your right-hand side. The path is faint as it traverses the fellside, and about 300m on, now with steep crags in front of you, it bends left to drop down, soon becoming more distinct and steeper and criss-crossing streams. About ¾ mile in all from the cairn, the path reaches a flat area with crags called Nitting Haws (NY 243 169).

4 The path bends left again here, and Grange now comes into view far below. For the next ¼ mile the path traverses the steep slopes – take care with children here as it is narrow – before giving way to a grassy descent and passing a cluster of large rocks. Further down you will hear and then see the network of streams coming down the fell called Greenup Sikes. At the bottom, the path reaches large and small wooden gates in a fence. Cross and then bear left, very soon passing a small water works building on your left (NY 247 176) and then cutting through bracken to a gate in a corner of two dry stone walls. Follow the clear path beyond for just over 200m and emerge via a gate at the road by the Borrowdale Gates hotel. Turn right for the village and car park.

Maiden Moor

1887'

from Rigg Beck

- Stair
  ▲ CATBELLS
- Little Town
- ▲ MAIDEN MOOR
  - Grange
- ▲ HIGH SPY
- Rosthwaite
  MILES
  0 1 2 3

from Scope End

NATURAL FEATURES

From mid-Newlands, Maiden Moor is seen to rise in three tiers: the lowest, rock-crowned, behind the hamlet of Little Town; the second, also craggy, above but some distance back; and finally the summit, set at the edge of a steep fall to the upper reaches of the valley. To the left of these successive steps is the wide hollow of Yewthwaite Comb, formerly a scene of mining activity but now a quiet sheep-pasture, below the slow decline of the summit-slope eastwards across a tilted plateau.

On the opposite side of the fell is the parallel valley of Borrowdale, to which Maiden Moor presents a steep slope of undistinguished appearance and a high level skyline, this being not the ridge but the plateau edge, the summit itself being out of sight.

Maiden Moor is the middle section of a very popular fellwalk, starting with Catbells and ending at Honister, along the spine of the ridge forming the Newlands and Borrowdale watershed. Both flanks are scarped — that facing Newlands almost continuously — so that, while the walk along the top is simple and pleasant, on grass, direct access from either valley is possible only in a few places without encountering rock.

The streams are small and insignificant; they drain into the River Derwent to the east and Newlands Beck to the west, joining, however, in the flat country before Bassenthwaite Lake.

1 : The summit
2 : High Crags
3 : Knott End
4 : Yewthwaite Comb
5 : Yewthwaite Mine
6 : Newlands Beck
7 : Yewthwaite Gill
8 : High Spy
9 : slope of Catbells

looking south

The entrance to Little Mine — one of two small mines opened on the lower slopes above Newlands, in view from the old road leading up the valley.

239

MAP

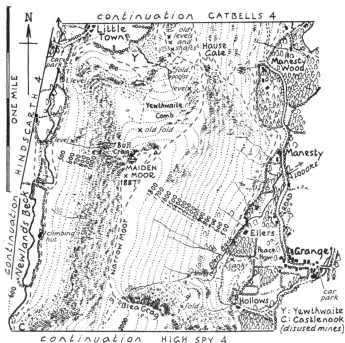

continuation CATBELLS 4

N

ONE MILE

HINDSCARTH 4

continuation Newlands Beck

Little Town

car park

L level

800

old x levels and x shafts

x fold pools

/level x

Hause Gate

Manesty Wood

Yewthwaite Comb

x old fold

Bull Crag

level

MAIDEN x MOOR 1887

800

Manesty

LODORE

ROAD

climbing hut

NARROW MOOR

1800 1700 1600

Ellers

Peace How

falls

tank

Hollows

Blea Crag

x fold

car park

continuation HIGH SPY 4

Y: Yewthwaite
C: Castlenook
(disused mines)

In the vicinity of Ellers.......

Peace How

Ellers Beck flows alongside the grounds of Ellers, a natural boundary being provided by a long wall of rock bordering the stream. The cave illustrated (right) – evidence of old mining activity – was in the rockface directly behind the house of Ellers. In 2008 it could not be found.

Bedecked with rhododendrons and watered by a sweet stream, this was Lakeland's most exotic cave.

ASCENTS FROM GRANGE
via MANESTY
1600 feet of ascent
2½ miles

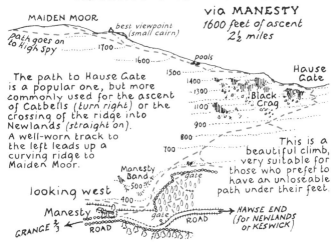

MAIDEN MOOR

best viewpoint (small cairn)

path goes on to High Spy

1700

1600

pools

1500

1400

1300

1100

900

800

700

Hause Gate

Black Crag

The path to Hause Gate is a popular one, but more commonly used for the ascent of Catbells (turn right) or the crossing of the ridge into Newlands (straight on).
A well-worn track to the left leads up a curving ridge to Maiden Moor.

This is a beautiful climb, very suitable for those who prefer to have an unloseable path under their feet.

looking west

Manesty Band

500

400

gate

gate

Manesty

GRANGE ⅔

ROAD

ROAD

HAWSE END (for NEWLANDS or KESWICK)

via PEACE HOW : 1600 feet of ascent : 2 miles

HIGH SPY

Blea Crag

Narrow Moor

MAIDEN MOOR

grass

1800

1600

heather

1300

Greenup

900

bracken

waterfalls

700

600

weir

500

Ellers Beck

400

There is no path above the falls. The final heathery slope is very much longer than it appears to be from below

For further details of this route see High Spy 6

As far as the waterfalls this walk is delightful, but then follows a tiring trudge up a steepening, uninteresting slope.

water tank

Swanesty How

Ellers

x seat

Peace How

Grange

MANESTY

looking west

ROAD

Hotel

Waterfalls above Ellers Beck

ASCENT FROM LITTLE TOWN
1250 feet of ascent : 1½ or 2 miles

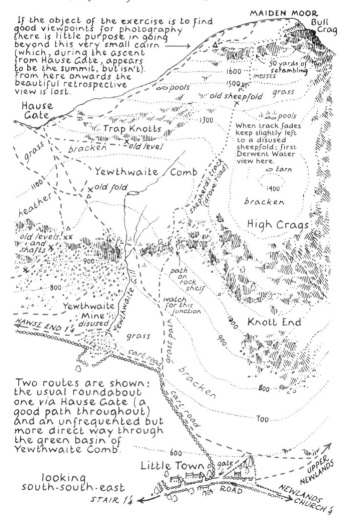

MAIDEN MOOR

Bull Crag

If the object of the exercise is to find good viewpoints for photography there is little purpose in going beyond this very small cairn (which, during the ascent from Hause Gate, appears to be the summit, but isn't). From here onwards the beautiful retrospective view is lost.

50 yards of scrambling
mosses
grass
1600
1500
old sheepfold
∞ pools

Hause Gate

1300

Trap Knotts
grass
bracken × old level

When track fades keep slightly left to a disused sheepfold; first Derwent Water view here.
∞ pools

Yewthwaite Comb

× old fold

○ tarn
1400

heather
1100
shepherd's track (drove road)
bracken
High Crags

old levels ×× and shafts ×
900

path on rock shelf

800
watch for this junction

Yewthwaite Mine disused

HAWSE END 1¼
grass
1000
Knott End
900

cart road
grass path
800

Two routes are shown: the usual roundabout one via Hause Gate (a good path throughout) and an unfrequented but more direct way through the green basin of Yewthwaite Comb.

bracken
cart road
700

600
gate
Little Town
UPPER NEWLANDS

looking south-south-east
STAIR 1¼
ROAD
NEWLANDS CHURCH ¾

242

THE SUMMIT

Short of lying down with eyes at ground level and taking a few elementary perspectives, there is no way by which a layman can determine the highest point of the fell — and although the Ordnance Survey have been on the spot with instruments and arrived at their own expert conclusions they have left no sign of their visit, and there is no cairn. The actual top could be anywhere within a twenty-yard radius. All is grassy and uninteresting here, without as much as a stone to sit on or an outcrop to recline against, but those who feel the ascent has merited a rest can take their reward on the edge of the steep drop into Newlands, just west of whatever is decided as the summit. A track follows this edge, but the main path across the moor runs some 200 yards to the east.

DESCENTS: Join the path referred to (you can't miss it, even in mist: it stands out from the grass as a dark grey ribbon of gravel) and follow it left down to Hause Gate for Newlands, left, or Borrowdale, right.

Bull Crag is bull-nosed, i.e. in profile it appears as a rounded overhang

The Newlands edge from the top of Bull Crag, looking south-west

THE VIEW

A dreary foreground detracts from the view and unfortunately hides Borrowdale and most of Derwent Water. In other respects the scene is satisfactory, and especially good looking north. A tiny cairn on the edge of the plateau to the north-east commands a much more beautiful though less extensive view.

Principal Fells

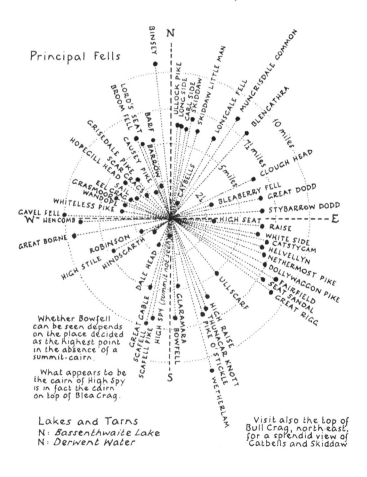

Whether Bowfell can be seen depends on the place decided as the highest point in the absence of a summit-cairn.

What appears to be the cairn of High Spy is in fact the cairn on top of Blea Crag.

Lakes and Tarns
N: *Bassenthwaite Lake*
N: *Derwent Water*

Visit also the top of Bull Crag, north-east, for a splendid view of Catbells and Skiddaw

RIDGE ROUTES

To CATBELLS, 1481′: 1½ miles : N.E, then N.

Depression (Hause Gate) at 1180′: 310 feet of ascent

It must be something like this in Heaven

Cross to the cairn on the north-east edge of the plateau (this is a notable viewpoint), reaching this preferably by keeping to the rim of the crags. A well-worn path now goes down in a curve to Hause Gate, whence a broad grass path leads easily upwards to Catbells. Beautiful views.

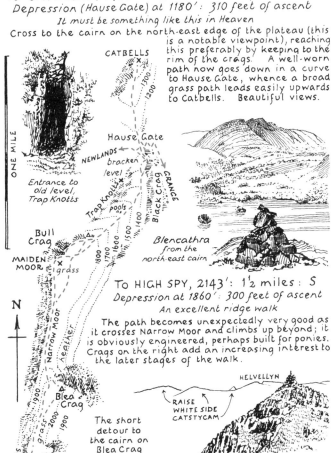

CATBELLS

1700

1200

Hause Gate

NEWLANDS

bracken level

GRANGE

Black

Trap Knotts

pools

1400

1500

1600

1700

1800

Entrance to old level, Trap Knotts

Bull Crag

MAIDEN MOOR × grass

N

Narrow Moor

heather

1900

Blea Crag

2000

1900

grass

Eel Crags

Minum Crag

▲ HIGH SPY

Blencathra from the north-east cairn

To HIGH SPY, 2143′: 1½ miles : S

Depression at 1860′: 300 feet of ascent

An excellent ridge walk

The path becomes unexpectedly very good as it crosses Narrow Moor and climbs up beyond; it is obviously engineered, perhaps built for ponies. Crags on the right add an increasing interest to the later stages of the walk.

HELVELLYN

RAISE

WHITE SIDE

CATSTYCAM

The short detour to the cairn on Blea Crag is strongly urged: here is one of the finest views of Derwent Water

The cairn on Blea Crag (the Helvellyn range in the background)

20 Place Fell
from Patterdale

Wainwright was not one to dish out compliments lightly, so his comments about Place Fell represent high praise indeed. 'No other viewpoint gives such an appreciation of the design of this lovely corner of Lakeland', he wrote. 'One cannot sojourn at Patterdale without looking at Place Fell and one cannot look long at Place Fell without duly setting forth to climb it. The time is very well spent.'

At more than 2,000 feet the fell is the highest in this book, but the extra effort required to reach its top is justified by Wainwright's enthusiasm and the wonderful views that are achieved. This walk follows Wainwright's suggested ascent from Patterdale – via Boredale Hause, the busy crossroads of paths that is a stopping point for the walk up to Angletarn Pikes in Chapter 13 of this book – but extends things by continuing on to Scalehow Force and Wood on the fringe of Ullswater. This enables a return to Patterdale along a path that clings close to the lake – a stretch which excited Wainwright even more than Place Fell itself. 'It is the author's opinion that the lakeside path ... is the most beautiful and rewarding walk in Lakeland.' From the man who trod just about every inch of it, this is the ultimate accolade.

The extra stretch along the lake brings the length of the walk to about 7 miles, but the paths are mostly straightforward and there are good spots to rest along the way. To cut the length in half but still incorporate Place Fell, simply return by the same way you climbed up, or divert left soon after the summit to descend on the Hare Shaw path; this eventually winds down to a track that runs parallel to and above the lakeside one, back to Patterdale. To extend the walk still further, continue on past Scalehow Wood to Sandwick and start the lakeside path from there.

From *Book Two: The Far Eastern Fells*

Distance 7 miles (11.2km)

Ascent 1,900 feet (580m)

Start and finish point The car park of the White Lion pub in Patterdale (NY 397 159)

Ordnance Survey maps Explorer OL5; Landranger 90

Getting there

Patterdale is at the foot of Ullswater on the A592, the road that bisects the Lake District from Penrith in the north to Bowness, Windermere and Newby Bridge in the south. The car park of the White Lion is on the left as you arrive in the village from the south. Once parked there, buy a ticket for the day from the pub across the road; the fee is fully refunded against food or drink purchases after your walk. There is alternative parking elsewhere in Patterdale, including some free roadside spots, but it is something of a free-for-all and spaces fill up very quickly.

Patterdale is well served by buses. The 108 service runs to Patterdale from Penrith, via Eamont Bridge, Tirril and Pooley Bridge, and starts from the town's train station, which is on the west coast main rail line. The more limited 508 service runs from Penrith but extends to Windermere and Bowness; it runs four times a day at weekends and on weekdays in the school summer holidays. The 208 bus also runs from Penrith, and then on from Patterdale to Keswick.

Facilities, food and drink

Patterdale has several places to eat, including the 19th century White Lion pub at the start and finish, which will make up packed lunches for walkers (017684 82214, www.thewhitelioninnpatterdale.co.uk); and the Patterdale Hotel, where the public bar is called the Place Fell Inn (0845 305 2111, www.patterdalehotel.co.uk). Side Farm, close to the end of the walk, has a nice tearoom (017684 82337). And the

Patterdale Village Store, between the White Lion car park and the pub itself, sells food and drink for picnics, plus very good Cumberland sausage baguettes (017684 82220).

There are more eating options a short drive north along the A592 in Glenridding, including the Travellers Rest pub (017684 82298) and the Glenridding Hotel (017684 82289, www.bw-glenriddinghotel.co.uk). The village offers rides across the lake with the Ullswater Steamers company (017684 82229, www.ullswater-steamers.co.uk), and you can hire boats to take out on the lake yourself at the Glenridding Sailing Centre (017684 82541, www.glenriddingsailingcentre.co.uk). There is a Tourist Information Centre in the village's main car park (017684 82414).

Directions

1 Turn right out of the car park to walk away from the village. Take a left turn by a Parish noticeboard to cross the river over Goldrill Bridge. Follow the narrow road up to a cluster of houses and bear left at a fork, following the signs for Boredale Hause. Rise up to another junction, and leave the road through a wooden gate on to a track, again signposted for Boredale Hause. After a couple of zig-zags the path splits; turn right. About 150m further on, at another junction, bear left and soon rise up to a green bench. The path now climbs steadily and then passes two small trees close together on your left. After the first of them, look for a path to the left that immediately zig-zags past the second. Follow this as it rises, passing a rough cairn and then meeting a junction of paths by a ruined sheepfold (NY 408 157). This is part of Boredale Hause, the broad intersection of paths to various fells and valleys.

2 Turn left at the junction on to the clear stony track, immediately passing another ruined sheepfold. This track now climbs again, and after a little under ½ mile turns left and narrows, rising again over flights of stone steps up to a crag. Most children will be able to scramble over this, though it can be skirted on a grassy path to the right. Once over it, the summit of Place Fell is in view ahead, and the path to it is clear and easy. The summit has a triangulation column and a cairn, and knolls and outcrops to explore (NY 406 170).

3 Continue on the path over the top, soon dropping down to pass a small tarn on your right, then rising up and over a craggy mound to a depression with a sheepfold, just under 1 mile from the summit (NY 414 179). Immediately after this, bear left to skirt to the left of the peak in front of you (High Dodd) rather than taking the route to the right of it. Just under ½ mile further on, having passed a disused quarry and a ruined building attached to it, and with part of Ullswater having appeared in view ahead, the path forks again (NY 413 185). Take the left-hand option on to a stony path in the direction of the lake, with Scalehow Beck soon joining you on your left. Just under ½ mile from this junction, by a large boulder, turn left on to a steep grassy path down towards a track visible beneath you. (If the path is too steep for you, carry on and curve down to it further on.)

4 Turn left along the track, immediately crossing Scalehow Beck on a footbridge and passing Scalehow Wood over the wall to your right, before Ullswater opens up gloriously. The path is completely clear as it winds and undulates alongside Ullswater, with plenty of picnic spots on the way. 1½ miles on from the footbridge, soon after exiting a long stretch of trees and with a broad bay, Silver Bay, down to your right, the path splits (NY 397 183). Do not take the stone steps to the left, but continue on the lower track. Soon after there is another fork; the right-hand grassy path takes you a short diversion to a fine viewing point on a crag, but otherwise continue for 1½ miles, the path clear throughout, to Side Farm (NY 398 163). Turn right through the farm buildings, which include a tearoom on your right, and follow the farm track down to Patterdale. At the main road, turn left for the White Lion car park.

Place Fell

2154'

from Birks

Few fells are so well favoured as Place Fell for appraising neighbouring heights. It occupies an exceptionally good position in the curve of Ullswater, in the centre of a great bowl of hills; its summit commands a very beautiful and impressive panorama. On a first visit to Patterdale, Place Fell should be an early objective, for no other viewpoint gives such an appreciation of the design of this lovely corner of Lakeland.

NATURAL FEATURES

Place Fell rises steeply from the curve formed by the upper and middle reaches of Ullswater and its bulky mass dominates the head of the lake. Of only moderate elevation, and considerably overtopped by surrounding heights, nevertheless the fell more than holds its own even in such a goodly company: it has that distinctive blend of outline and rugged solidity characteristic of the true mountain. Many discoveries await those who explore: in particular the abrupt western flank, richly clothed with juniper and bracken and heather, and plunging down to the lake in a rough tumble of crag and scree, boulders and birches, is a paradise for the scrambler, while a more adventurous walker will find a keen enjoyment in tracing the many forgotten and overgrown paths across the fellside and in following the exciting and airy sheep-tracks that so skilfully contour the steep upper slopes below the hoary crest.

The eastern face, overlooking Boredale, is riven by deepcut gullies and is everywhere steep. Northward two ridges descend more gradually to the shores of Ullswater after passing over minor summits; from a lonely hollow between them issues the main stream on the fell, Scalehow Beck, which has good waterfalls. To the south, Boredale Hause is a well-known walkers' crossroads, and beyond this depression high ground continues to climb towards the principal watershed.

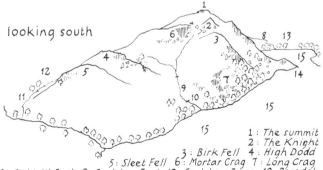

looking south

1 : The summit
2 : The Knight
3 : Birk Fell 4 : High Dodd
5 : Sleet Fell 6 : Mortar Crag 7 : Long Crag
8 : Goldrill Beck 9 : Scalehow Beck 10 : Scalehow Force 12 : Boredale
11 : Boredale Beck 13 : Patterdale 14 : Silver Point 15 : Ullswater

MAP

It is the author's opinion that the lakeside path from Scalehow Beck, near Sandwick, to Patterdale (in that direction) is the most beautiful and rewarding walk in Lakeland.
The junction of paths at Silver Bay is marked by a large cairn.

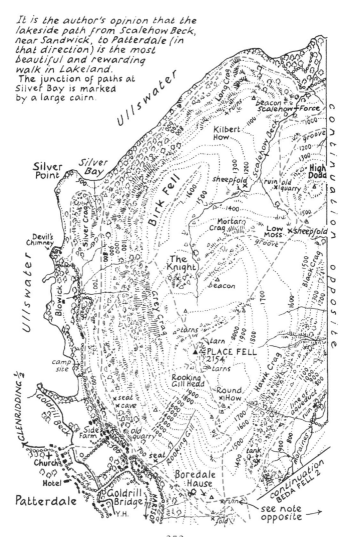

252

MAP

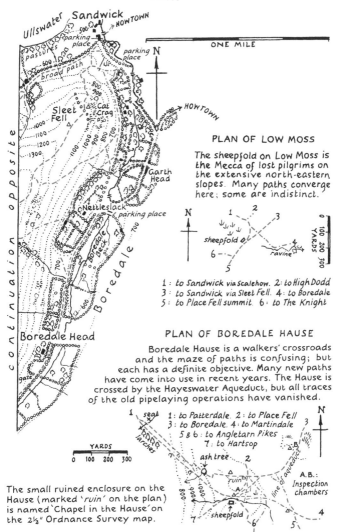

ONE MILE

PLAN OF LOW MOSS

The sheepfold on Low Moss is the Mecca of lost pilgrims on the extensive north-eastern slopes. Many paths converge here; some are indistinct.

1: to Sandwick via Scalehow. 2: to High Dodd
3: to Sandwick via Sleet Fell. 4: to Boredale
5: to Place Fell summit. 6: to The Knight

PLAN OF BOREDALE HAUSE

Boredale Hause is a walkers' crossroads and the maze of paths is confusing; but each has a definite objective. Many new paths have come into use in recent years. The Hause is crossed by the Hayeswater Aqueduct, but all traces of the old pipelaying operations have vanished.

1: to Patterdale. 2: to Place Fell
3: to Boredale. 4: to Martindale
5 & 6: to Angletarn Pikes
7: to Hartsop

A.B.: Inspection chambers

The small ruined enclosure on the Hause (marked 'ruin' on the plan) is named 'Chapel in the Hause' on the 2½" Ordnance Survey map.

ASCENT FROM PATTERDALE
1700 feet of ascent : 1¾ miles

The face of Place Fell overlooking Patterdale is unremittingly and uncompromisingly steep, and the ascent is invariably made by way of the easier gradients of Boredale Hause, there being a continuous path on this route. (*From the valley there appear to be paths going straight up the fell, but these are not paths at all: they are incipient streams and runnels.*) As an alternative, an old neglected track that branches from the higher path to Silver Bay is recommended: this slants leftwards to the skyline depression between Birk Fell and Grey Crag. This old track is difficult to locate from above and is better not used for descent as there is rough ground in the vicinity.

The diversion of the old track from the higher path to Silver Bay occurs a full half-mile beyond the quarry at a point where there is a bluff of grey rock on the left above some larches. A flat boulder marks the junction, and a few ancient cairns along the route are also a help. Botanists will find much of interest here.

Note also, 200 yards up the old track, a faint path turning away on the right: this climbs high across the face below Grey Crag, is lost on scree, but can be traced beyond, on the 1500' contour, all the way to the usual route *via* Boredale Hause—an exhilarating high-level walk. From this path the summit may be gained without difficulty *after* leaving Grey Crag behind and crossing a small ravine.

On the Boredale Hause route, take the upper path at the fork near the seat. Watch for the zig-zag: if this is missed the walker naturally gravitates to the lower path. The striking ash tree is on the *upper* path.

One cannot sojourn at Patterdale without looking at Place Fell and one cannot look long at Place Fell without duly setting forth to climb it. The time is very well spent.

ASCENT FROM SANDWICK
1700 feet of ascent : 2½ miles

Of the two routes shown from
Low Moss to the summit,
the one on the left
is *very much*
the better.

PLACE FELL

Top of Grey Crag

The Knight

grass · beacon

groove · Mortar Crag

Low Moss
sheepfold

grass

Birk Fell

BOREDALE HAUSE

ravine

High Dodd
ruin

sheepfold

Scalehow Beck

beacon

←path choked with bracken in summer

groove

groove

Scalehow Force

PATTERDALE 3

barn

bracken

Sleet Fell

old wall

Nettleslack

←path starts 10 yards past double bend in wall

barn

Boredale Beck

bracken

barn

Ullswater

seat

broad path

signpost

HOWTOWN 1½

parking place

Sandwick Beck

parking place

Sandwick

HOWTOWN 1¾

looking south-west

Five alternatives are shown
for the initial part of the climb,
the best on a clear day being over
the top of Sleet Fell (which is steep).
All ways converge near the sheepfold on
Low Moss, beyond which is a further choice.

THE SUMMIT
A rocky ridge overtops gently-rising
slopes and has a cairn at one end and
a triangulation column at the other.
There is a better cairn farther north.

DESCENTS : Routes of descent are indicated in the illustration
of the view; that to Boredale Hause is safest in bad weather.

THE VIEW

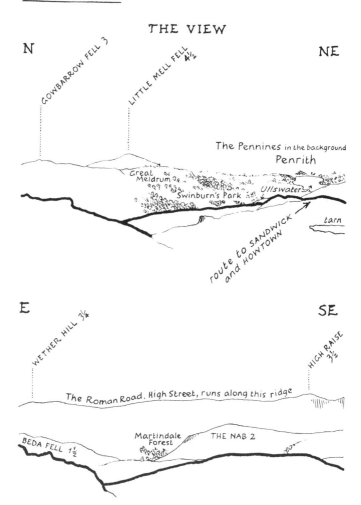

The thick line marks the visible boundaries
of Place Fell from the summit·cairn.
    The figures following the names of fells
    indicate distances in miles.

THE VIEW

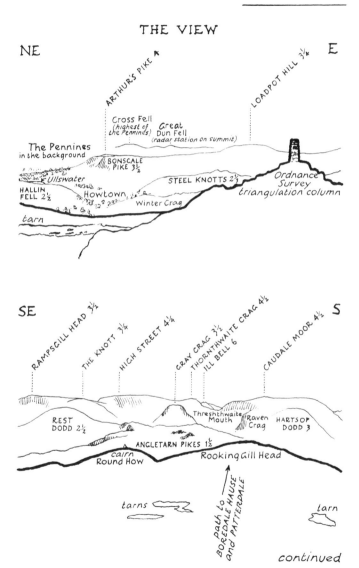

NE · E

ARTHUR'S PIKE ▲

Cross Fell
(highest of
the Pennines)

Great
Dun Fell
(radar station on summit)

LOADPOT HILL 3¾

The Pennines
in the background

BONSCALE
PIKE 3½

Ullswater

HALLIN
FELL 2½

Howtown

Winter Crag

STEEL KNOTTS 2⅓

Ordnance
Survey
triangulation column

tarn

SE · S

RAMPSGILL HEAD 3½

THE KNOTT 3¾

HIGH STREET 4¼

GRAY CRAG 3½

THORNTHWAITE CRAG 4½

ILL BELL 6

CAUDALE MOOR 4½

REST
DODD 2½

Threshthwaite
Mouth

Raven
Crag

HARTSOP
DODD 3

ANGLETARN PIKES 1½

cairn
Round How

Rooking Gill Head

Path to
BOREDALE HAUSE
and PATTERDALE

tarns

tarn

continued

257

THE VIEW

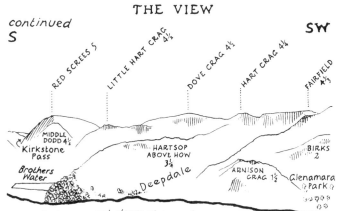

continued
S

SW

RED SCREES S

LITTLE HART CRAG 4½

DOVE CRAG 4½

HART CRAG 4¾

FAIRFIELD 4⅓

MIDDLE DODD 4½
Kirkstone Pass

Brothers Water

HARTSOP ABOVE HOW 3¼

Deepdale

ARNISON CRAG 1½

BIRKS 2

Glenamara Park

A steep, rough descent may be made to Patterdale
over this edge, but there is no path. The Boredale
Hause route is to be preferred, and takes no longer

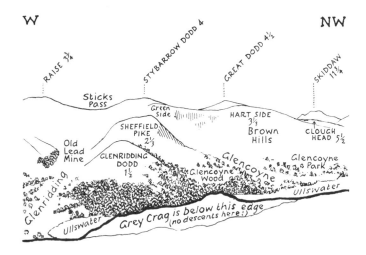

W

NW

RAISE 3¾

STYBARROW DODD 4

GREAT DODD 4½

SKIDDAW 11½

Sticks Pass

Green Side

HART SIDE 3⅓

CLOUGH HEAD 5½

SHEFFIELD PIKE 2⅓

Brown Hills

Old Lead Mine

GLENRIDDING DODD 1½

Glencoyne

Glencoyne Wood

Glencoyne Park

Glenridding

Ullswater

Ullswater

Grey Crag is below this edge (no descents here!)

THE VIEW

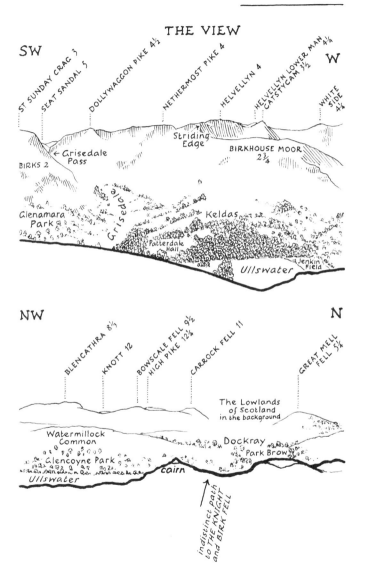

SW

St Sunday Crag 3
Seat Sandal 5
Dollywaggon Pike 4½
Nethermost Pike 4
Helvellyn 4
Helvellyn Lower Man 4¼
Catstycam 3½
White Side 4¼

W

← Grisedale Pass
Striding Edge
Birkhouse Moor 2¾

BIRKS 2

Glenamara Park

Grisedale

Keldas

Patterdale Hall

Ullswater

Jenkin Field

NW

Blencathra 8⅓
Knott 12
Bowscale Fell 9½
High Pike 12¼
Carrock Fell 11
Great Mell Fell 5¼

N

The Lowlands of Scotland in the background

Watermillock Common

Dockray
Park Brow

Glencoyne Park

Ullswater

cairn

Indistinct path to THE KNIGHT and BIRK FELL

259

INDEX
Main entries are in **bold**

Angle Tarn 164–5
Angletarn Pikes **164–75**, 246
Applethwaite 122
Ard Crags 23
Askham 210, 211
Askill Knott 192

Barrow **80–91**
Barrow Gill 83
Bassenthwaite 9, 32, 33–4, 56, 58–9, 83, 92, 93, 95
Bewaldeth 57, 58
Binsey 9, **56–67**
Black Beck 218, 220
Blackbeck Tarn 218, 220
Bleaberry Fell 200
Blencathra 17
Boredale 15
Boredale Hause 164, 166–7, 246, 248
Borrowdale 9, 10, 110–12
Bowder Stone 69, 71, 235, 236
Braithwaite 80, 81–3, 137
Bull Crag 237
Buttermere 23–4, 48, 49–51, 192, 219, 220

Castle Crag 10, **110–21**
Cat Gill 203
Catbells 9, **176–89**, 234, 236
Causey Pike 22, **136–49**
Cockermouth 34, 192
Cockpit, 210, 213
Coleridge, Samuel 7
Cop Stone 210, 211, 213
Crabtree Beck 193
Crummock Water 48, 49, 50, 51, 150, 192

Dale Head 234
Darling Fell 190, 193
Derwent Water 83, 122, 124, 138, 176, 200, 202, 236
Derwent, River 70, 110
Dodd **92–109**
Dodd Wood 59

Edward VII 68, 71
Embleton 34

Force Crag Mine 81

Gatesgarth 218, 219–20
Glenridding 16–17, 166, 248
Grange 68, 69–70, 111, 112, 176, 234, 235
Grange Fell (King's How) **68–79**
Greenup Sikes 237
Greta, River 123

Hallin Fell 11, **14–21**
Hare Shaw 246
Harris Park 34
Hause Gate 177, 179, 236
Hawse End 176, 177–9
Haystacks 10, 24, 50, **218–33**
Helvellyn 17
Heughscar Hill **210–17**
High Dodd 249
High Spy 48, 110, 234
High Street 165, 210
Honister Slate Mine 112, 220
Howtown 15, 16–17

Innominate Tarn 218
Ireby 58

Jesty, Chris 9

Keskadale 23

Keswick 9, 24, 34, 70, 80, 81, 112, 122–5, 138, 176, 177–9, 200–2, 235, 236
Kinder Scout 122
King's How 9
Knott Rigg **22–31**

Latrigg 9, **122–35**
Little Round How 221
Lodore Falls 236
Low Bank 49, 51
Low Fell 9, 150, **190–9**
Loweswater 9, 150–2, 190, 191–2, 193
Lowther Estate 212

Maiden Moor 177, **234–45**
Manesty 234, 235, 236
Martindale 14, 15–16
Mellbreak 9, **150–63**, 190
Mirehouse 92, 93, 94
Moor Divock 210
Mosedale 150
Moss Force 24–5

Narrow Moor 237
Newlands Hause 22, 23–4, 25
Nitting Haws 237

Outerside 81
Outlying Fells of Lakeland 9, 210

Patterdale 17, 164, 165–6, 246, 247–9
Penrith 210, 211
Pictorial Guides to the Lakeland Fells 7–8, 9, 12, 14, 23, 32, 57, 92, 110, 122
Place Fell 10, 11, 164, **246–59**
Pooley Bridge 15–16
Portinscale 24, 138
Potter, Beatrix 138, 176, 234

Rannerdale Knotts **48–55**
Red Pike 48
Robinson 48
Rosthwaite 70, 110–13, 236
Routenbeck 35
Rowling End 136
Ruskin, John 7

Sail 81
Sale Fell 9, **32–47**
Sandwick 15
Scalehow 246, 249
Scarth Gap 218, 220–1
Seatoller 112
Silver Bay 249
Size, Nicholas 48
Skiddaw 123
Skill Beck 95
Sleet Hause 136, 139
Stair 24, 136, 137, 138
Starling Dodd 8
Stonethwaite 70, 111, 112
Stonycroft Gill 139

Uldale 58
Ullswater 10, 14, 15, 17, 210, 246, 249

Wainwright, Alfred 7–8, 9, 10, 11, 12, 14, 17, 22, 32, 48, 50, 57, 68, 80, 92, 110, 122, 136, 164, 176, 190–1, 200, 210, 234, 246
Walla Crag **200–9**
Warnscale Beck 218
Waterend 191
West Crag 59
Whinlatter Forest 80, 81
Wordsworth, William 7, 34
Wythop 33–5